Mattie

Mattie
A Woman's Journey West

by Nan Weber

HOMESTEAD PUBLISHING
Moose, WY & San Francisco, CA

ISBN 0-943972-42-6
Library of Congress Catalog Card Number 95-81342
Printed in the United States of America
on recycled, acid free paper.
3 5 7 9 10 8 6 4 2

Published by
HOMESTEAD PUBLISHING
Box 193, Moose, Wyoming 83012
& San Francisco, CA

Contents

Dedicated to

*Becky and Pat Pitman who, during their lifetimes,
shared my joy and enthusiasm for hiking old trails
and piecing together old dishes that had been part of past lives.*

Acknowledgments

I would like to thank the following people who helped bring Mattie's story to life: Freda Beach, who gave me invaluable family insight into "Uncle Ellery," as well as the photo of Ellery in old age, and his obituary; Howard (Chris) Christiansen, grandnephew of Bernie Stamp, who shared memories of Lida Shipley Stamp; Edwin Jelsing, subsequent owner of the Alston house in Spokane, Washington, who gave me Mattie's autograph book, Ellery Culver's Civil War letters, Theda Culver's school work, family photos, and remembrances of the sale of the house; Heidi Jelsing, Edwin's granddaughter, who sent me Mattie's, Theda's and "Mother's" napkin rings, the photo of the Alston house in Spokane, and Grace Alston Hedrick's diaries.

Bernice Matthews, county clerk in Miles City, Montana, who took extra time and effort to locate Mattie's court case and then let me spend all day with the documents to read, digest and copy; Dick Pace, late Virginia City, Montana historian, who dug up many references to events in Ellery's life; Doris Whithorn, Livingston, Montana historian, who not only came up with Ellery's 1895 photo, but also pulled tons of tidbits about him from the Livingston and Gardiner newspapers; Aubrey Haines, historian, who unselfishly shared photos of Ellery, Mattie's grave, modes of transportation in Yellowstone Park and oral interviews about Ellery, and who also gave me invaluable support and encouragement.

Walter Hickey, Lowell, Massachusetts historian, who helped me analyze the economic situation of Mattie's family in Lowell, gave me data about the mills, and located the family in various sources; head ranger at Lowell Historical National Park, who arranged a private tour of the mills for me and started up the machinery to run the looms—what a wonderful way to experience what mill workers did; Barbara Zafft, librarian at Yellowstone National Park, who took me into the library and definitely went the extra mile to help me follow up all my "leads"; Joann Armstrong, communication specialist for District No. 81 of the Spokane Public Schools who, without notice, made me at home in her office and found school records for me to pore through; and all the good samaritans who helped me in courthouses, libraries, archives, cemeteries, newspaper offices and national parks and never stayed around long enough to give me their names.

My very special thanks to: my husband Paul Boruff, helpmate and traveling companion, who was with me every step of the way via snowmobile, car and on foot; Georgia Weber, genealogist extraordinaire, who helped me with everything from beginning research to editing this book; Carol Klumpp, who gave me emotional encouragement; Lavera Boruff for her love and financial support; my publisher, Carl Schreier, for believing in this project from the beginning, and editor Diane Henderson for her patience and expertise.

Introduction

Wandering innocently through Yellowstone National Park, I stumbled upon the gravesite of Mattie Shipley Culver. That was 1984, the first year I was living and working in West Yellowstone, Montana. During the next few years, my unanswered questions about Mattie got the better of me. In 1987, I began my quest for the woman who was Mattie Culver. Throughout the course of my research, I was fortunate enough to be given some of her personal possessions. These pieces of Mattie's past have helped me, not only to uncover her personal history, but also to recognize just how strong a woman she had to be to live in the Yellowstone region and to work in the textile industry of New York in the 1800s. Mattie's experiences helped me discover the strengths that we must possess as humans, and as women.

I would like to introduce the Mattie I have come to know. This is the history of a seemingly ordinary woman—not someone rich or famous, not an activist or trend setter. This is the story of a woman trying to better her life—leaving her mark, whether she knew it or not.

Sometimes we may think we are alone in the world, but the truth is that we affect and are affected by everyone around us and are part of a bigger picture. Mattie certainly was. And because her spirited life led her to Yellowstone National Park, she continues to influence people even today.

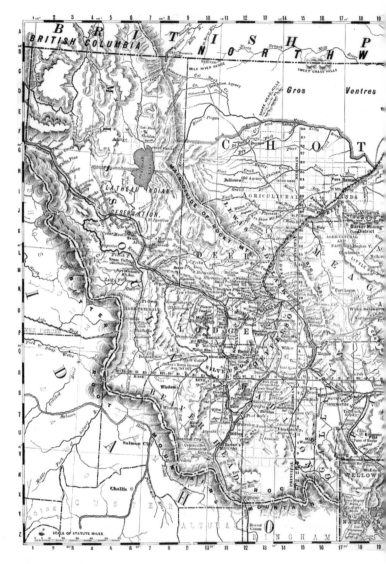

MONTANA TERRITORY, 1888

This Rand, McNally & Co. map depicts Montana Territory as it existed shortly after Mattie Shipley Culver moved West from New York. Newberry Library, Chicago, Illinois.

Mattie
A Woman's Journey West

Chapter 1

Discovering Mattie

single rose is carved into the white, Italian marble
tombstone. It's an elegant, solitary gravesite, on a strip
of land between Nez Perce Creek and the Firehole
River, in Yellowstone National Park. The
inscription below the rose marks its remembrance: Mattie S., wife of E.C. Culver, died March 2, 1889, aged 30 years.
On the base, it professes, "The Pure in
Heart shall see God."

*Gravesite of Mattie S. Culver in
Yellowstone Park. Photo courtesy
of The Schreier Collection.*

I happened upon the gravesite the
same way thousands of people do each
year. While I was stopped at the Nez
Perce picnic area off Fountain Flat Drive,
I decided to explore the river bank. Behind the outhouse there, the land rises a bit
before sweeping down to the grassy bank
of the Firehole River. On this rise is Mattie's
grave. It is protected by a series of old
wooden posts, held together with a brown
pipe railing to keep buffalo from trampling it. Although pictur-
esque, it seemed an unlikely place for a grave. Who was Mattie S.,
and why was she buried here? I looked around. There was nothing to tell her story, except for the few words on the tombstone.

I returned home to the gate town of West Yellowstone, never imagining how far my questions about Mattie would lead me in the end. I asked almost everyone in town about the woman buried in the park. They all seemed to have the same answer: "She was the wife of the winterkeeper of the old Firehole Hotel. She died in childbirth." That was all anyone seemed to know about Mattie.

At the time, I was relatively unfamiliar with Yellowstone's history but was fascinated with the thought of a hotel having been at the spot where Mattie was buried, and I was curious about it. Numerous people suggested that I read Aubrey Haines' *The Yellowstone Story*. Haines was the Yellowstone historian from 1959 to 1969 and, before that, held several other positions in the park. His work was said to be a comprehensive history and to include information about Mattie and her husband, E.C. Culver.

The Yellowstone Story did answer some of my questions about E.C. Culver and about the Firehole Hotel. But Mattie was still "the woman who died in childbirth"—that was it. Nonetheless, I felt sure that *someone* knew something about Mattie and that I eventually would find them. Meantime, I gathered what information I could about the hotel and the people associated with it. And I learned that E.C. Culver's first name was Ellery.

From the first day I saw her grave, Mattie had a hold on me. I kept returning to Fountain Flat Drive to explore. I was fascinated with the broken pieces of hotel china that lay at the bottom of the Firehole River. Did Mattie use that china? Who decided to toss the pieces into the river when they were broken?

I began taking flowers to the grave whenever I was in that part of the park. Later, I would discover that I was just one of many locals and summer employees offering this tribute; hundreds were drawn to the gravesite to "claim" Mattie as their own lost relative.

The trails that went to and from the old hotel site swept me into a hiking frenzy. My favorite was the old Fountain Freight Trail that heads over the Madison Plateau. An 1880s travel diary described the wagon trip that began at an area referred to as "Riverside" on the Madison River. When I hiked, I often imagined myself walking the seven miles to the summit in a heavy skirt. Or perhaps I would be like the women who were bold enough to sport the new "bloomer suits." That view of the geyser basins from above the Firehole Basin must have been breathtaking—much more dramatic than what the modern road offers.

Every time I took a bike trip toward Old Faithful, Mattie's gravesite served as a good stopping point for lunch. Watching mountain bluebirds feed their young in the nest they had fashioned in one of the support posts around the tombstone was always a highlight of my day. During these stopovers, I began hearing what I now call the "Mattie myths." People would gather at the gravesite—one, two or three at a time—and share what they had heard about Mattie.

One woman told me that relatives still visit the grave and that the daughter returned until the 1950s. One man was sure that Mattie was on a wagon train going through the park when she died. I also heard that Mattie's body was stored either on the roof of the hotel or in two pickle barrels, end to end, until she could be buried, and that Ellery stayed awake endlessly to guard her body from predators. Another woman told me that Ellery had to care for the baby alone so he fed her elk's milk. I immediately had striking visions of Ellery milking an elk. That was about all I could take. Truth and myth had to be separated, so I began formal research.

Research was not new to me. My sister, Georgia, a genealogist, started me off when I was about sixteen years old, digging up our family history. I discovered that the key to the past opens so many doors to the future. Women's history became my favorite, and theatre was my love, so living history, or first-person interpretation, became my performing specialty. Uncovering Mattie's life story certainly would fine tune these skills.

The hunt began with bits and pieces of Mattie's life, like the warp and weft of a tapestry. Women's history sometimes is difficult. Records of women's lives—especially in the 1800s—often are of a more personal nature than a civil one. Women's rights varied from state to state and certainly were not what they are today. Often, if a woman or her husband did not own land or property, she could become very obscure, if not completely lost, to future generations. Home sources—personal items that document someone's life—usually are rich with women's history. These items can be anything from Bible records, diaries and photos to quilts, artwork or toys.

To find out about Mattie's life, I began by trying to document her death. But there was no record of it at Park Service headquarters in Mammoth Hot Springs, and I went on to find that her death was not recorded in Wyoming or Montana at all. My luck didn't change when I tried to find a record of the birth of Mattie and Ellery's child. The child who was "fed on elk's milk" did not exist in civil records.

Then I remembered hearing that Mattie and Ellery's child was sent to Spokane, Washington, to live with Ellery's sister. If Mattie's child did survive to the 1950s to visit her mother's gravesite, then she should be in the 1900 census in Washington state.

What I found in the census schedule would serve as a springboard: Theda Culver, listed as a niece in the David Alston family

in Spokane, was the only Culver child I could locate in that area. Theda Culver, it said, was born in Montana in June, 1887 (see appendix, page 127). If Mattie had died while giving birth to this girl, the birth date must

The Alston home at W. 903 Chelan in Spokane, Washington.

have been recorded incorrectly in the census, because Mattie died in 1889. Or perhaps this was an older child and the child born in the park had died before the census. Now I was desperate to figure things out.

The whole Alston family was curious to me. I had some background about Ellery Culver's family and knew they were from Vermont. This family in Spokane didn't seem to be Ellery's sister's. Perhaps it was Mattie's sister's family. According to the census, Millie Alston, David's wife, was born in September, 1847 in England and immigrated to the United States in 1848. Theda Culver's mother also was born in England. Millie and David had three children, two born in Montana and one born in Washington. Finally, the household included a sister, Lida Shipley, single, born in October, 1858 in Massachusetts. If this was David's sister, she would be an Alston, not a Shipley. The tombstone in Yellowstone reads "Mattie S." If my speculation was correct, I had found Mattie's family.

Tracking Theda Culver's movements could help determine who her parents were. In the 1910 census, Theda no longer was listed as a member of the Alston household. Millie had been widowed between 1900 and 1910. Meanwhile, Lida Shipley had married a Mr. Stamp and also was widowed but continued to live in the Alston home. As I perused the death records in Spokane to see what had happened to David Alston, I was surprised to come across a death certificate for Theda Culver.[1]

Theda Culver died of a pulmonary edema at Washington Hospital on July 20, 1906, at the age of nineteen. So the 1900 census was correct in listing her birthdate as 1887. The death record identified her parents as Mattie Shipley and E.C. Culver. I was on my way to discovering Mattie's past!

Theda was buried in Fairmount Cemetery in Spokane on July 21, 1906.[2] The burial records indicated that Ellery Culver was born in Vermont and that Mattie was from New York. The information in the records had been provided by Ellery Culver.

Theda Culver was buried on the Alston plot in Fairmount Cemetery, Spokane, Washington.

Next, I hoped to locate descendants of the Alston family to help me trace Mattie further. Little did I know that I was about to find the key to Mattie's past and begin an odyssey that would take years to complete.

I was able to track David and Millie's eldest daughter, Grace, through the city directories. Though she moved to other residences for a time, Grace mainly lived with her mother, Millie, at W. 903 Chelan. Even after she married Ernest Hedrick, Grace was easily traceable up until 1955. Ernest was listed in the directories until 1958. When his name disappeared from the rosters, I used the address index to locate the next owner of the house—Edwin Jelsing. A quick check of the current phone book amazed me—it was thirty years later and Edwin Jelsing still lived there!

I wrote Mr. Jelsing a letter, explaining the research I was doing about Mattie, on the off-chance that he—or someone else in the neighborhood—would know something about the Hedricks or Alstons.

Luck was on my side. About a week and a half after I wrote to Mr. Jelsing, I received a package in the mail from Spokane. As my husband, Paul, will attest, I had a hard time keeping my feet on the ground. Following is the letter—original spelling retained—that accompanied the package. Mr. Jelsing's unselfish response furnished me with tangible pieces of Mattie's past:

> Dear Nan Waber
> Shur was A serpriss to get A letter From Salt Lake City. No we did not know Ernest H. We were looking for a place to buy. We happen to stop by this place.
> Asked if he would sell. After a few more stops. We made A dail an bought it.
> "Ja" tears came to his eyes. when he syned the papers. sead he was Married in frount of the big window. there is no one in this neighborhood that remember him. All the old people are gone.
> Am sending you some stuff that we found here hope it will be of some help.
> Sorry for the deley. Hope you can understand it.
> As ever Ed.

I ripped open the package and found an old-looking cardboard box, with the inscription, "Patsy's Original Candies From the Foot of Pikes Peak." Beneath those words was a drawing of a person cranking an old-fashioned taffy machine. It struck me as more than a coincidence because, for several summers, I had been working at a small candy store in West Yellowstone making taffy. So this package definitely "spoke" to me.

The box contained Civil War letters from Ellery to his sister,

Thede. Also included were numerous photographs—pictures of people in front of houses, by cars (1911 to 1930 vintages), next to trains, and sitting on the steps of a porch, plus several pictures of trains and train wrecks, school-type portraits, and pictures of children. None of the photographs were labeled. Correspondence between Grace Alston Hedrick and her brother, Edward, traced his movements until his death in California in 1938. Samples of Theda Culver's and Grace Alston's school work, marriage information about Grace Alston, church-membership information of Mildred Alston, and last—

and best of all—Mattie Shipley's autograph book, with autographs dating from 1878 to 1883, drew together pieces of the puzzle.

Even before I opened the reddish-brown autograph book, I sensed that it would reveal the life and world of Mattie Shipley. I felt honored to page through it, unveiling the people who called her friend. Now I would begin to break through those "Mattie myths."

I carefully followed every lead in the box to locate descendants of Millie and David Alston. Grace and Ernest Hedrick had no children. The Alstons' other daughter, Mildred, died of pneumonia in 1916, and their son, Edward, died in 1938. Both were

This picture likely is of Edward Shipley Alston.

single. Anxiously studying the features on the faces in the photographs, I was able to follow one face through several time periods. I presume this to be Grace Alston Hedrick because she was the family member who remained in the house on Chelan. I also believe that one of the pictures is of Edward Shipley Alston.

After much comparison and study of costume, I presumed

who the people in the photos might be. The only positive identi-
fication I have made is of Theda Culver, from her high-school
graduation photo in the *Spokane Daily Chronicle* of May 26, 1905.
The next two portraits, taken at the Maxwell studio in Spokane,
might have been posed for at the same sitting, in perhaps 1895
or 1896. The two school girls are the cousins who grew up together, Theda Culver on the left and Mildred Alston on the right.
The single photo (in grade-school graduation dress, possibly)

*The schoolgirls, above, are Theda Culver, left, and prob-
ably Mildred Alston. Grace Alston, in photo on right,
attended Bancroft Elementary School in Spokane. Her
Aunt Lida Shipley taught fifth grade there.*

*What likely is Grace
Alston in two more
photographs, left, in
what might be a high-
school graduation por-
trait, and right, an
older Grace on front
steps with two other
women.*

would be Mildred's older sister, Grace. Notice the similarities of
the sisters—the wide-set eyes, the long noses and the dainty de-
meanor.

The woman in the graduation dress, who I believe is Grace,
also appears in two other photos. The next portrait was one of

eight oval portraits of young females, pasted back-to-back. This likely was Grace's high-school graduation photo, and the other women some of her classmates. Grace graduated from Spokane High School in June, 1901. Holding true to family tradition, she then graduated from the training school in June, 1903[3] and began teaching first grade at Bancroft Elementary School. An older "Grace" is found in another picture—sitting on the steps with two other women.

---

[1] Register of Deaths, Spokane County, Washington, 1891-1907.

[2] Funeral Home Records, Smith's of Spokane, Washington, Vol. II, 1890-1906.

[3] School District No. 81, Spokane, Washington.

Chapter 2

Looming Passages

*M*attie's autograph book gave my research new direction. Now I focused both on the early part of her life in
New York and her later days in Montana.

New pieces of the puzzle began to meld when I located Freda
Beach, a descendant of one of Ellery's sisters. Freda said she didn't
really know anything about Mattie, except that she had the name
"Mattie Shipley Gillett" when she married "Uncle Ellery." Freda
knew more than she imagined. She had fed me a wonderful new
piece of information—the name *Gillett*. It suggested that Mattie
had been married to someone else before Ellery Culver. Even
more exciting was the obituary Freda sent me. Besides describ-
ing Ellery's last days, it also contained a firsthand account of
Mattie's death and burial.

I sent for Ellery's military records, knowing that he fought in
the Civil War. Meantime, I absorbed Mattie's autograph book,
which brought to life colorful places in New York—Cohoes,
Waterford, West Troy, Schenectady, Northside. But the place
mentioned most was Cohoes, so that's where I began. Poring
over a history from the time Mattie lived in Cohoes, I found
reference to a George Shipley serving in the Civil War and sent
for his military papers as well.

The records were full of information. They verified that George
Shipley was Mattie's father and revealed that Mattie's mother was

Elizabeth "Betty" Higgins. Now I had a birthplace for Mattie and all her brothers and sisters. I also learned where in England Betty and George came from. Exploring the English census records, I even found where Mattie's parents lived with *their* parents.

Both families were wrapped in the fabric of mill life—weaving and cotton factories. They were from Newton, Cheshire, England. Cheshire and Lancaster counties were the heart of the textile industry in England, and cotton weaving was Newton's claim to fame. George Shipley and his father both were weavers. Mattie's mother, Betty Higgins, also was a cotton weaver, and all of Betty's brothers and sisters worked in

Loom operators in mid-1800s. Mattie's family made its way working in weaving and cotton factories. The Cotton Industry, Chris Aspin, Shire Publications, Ltd.

the cotton mills in Newton. When Betty was still in her teens, her father died, leaving her mother to raise the family.

When George Shipley met Betty Higgins, Newton was a township of about 7,500 people. After the banns were published and read in the Parish Church and no objections were raised, George and Betty, both twenty-two, were married on Christmas Day in 1843. The ceremony was performed by D. Seddon, vicar of the Established Church at Mottram, Cheshire, England.

On October 10, 1844, George and Betty's first child, William Sidney Shipley, was born in Newton. They continued working while raising their son, but times were hard in the textile industry. Still, they were full of hope and were delighted when Betty delivered their first daughter, Pamela Ann "Millie," on September 13, 1847.

Shortly after George and Betty were married, Betty's younger sister, Martha, met James Platt. James was the son of a spinner-turned-grocer, from Mottram. Martha and James married and, soon after, emigrated to the United States. James' mother, sister and one brother left England with them. By 1848, they all settled in the textile center of Lowell, Massachusetts, on the Merrimack

River. James worked as a blacksmith for the Merrimack Corporation, one of the largest employers in Lowell.

In England, the textile industry was flourishing for factory owners, but the working conditions were deteriorating. It was common for immigrants, finding better working and living conditions, to encourage family members in the old country to join them in the United States.

Like all young parents, George and Betty wanted the best for their growing family, so they decided to join Martha and her family in the United States. On May 3, 1849, the ship John Currier sailed into Boston Harbor with George, Betty and their two young children among its passengers.

The Shipley family joined the Platts in Lowell. Even back in England, Lowell was known as a model textile town, the "City of Spindles."[1] Here, George and Betty hoped to raise their family in comfort. But competition from other New England textile cities threatened Lowell's prosperity. The problem that had plagued the English textile industry also had descended on Lowell; the mill owners would have to increase production to remain competitive.

So the Shipleys were entering a work environment similar to the one from which they had just escaped. At one of the major corporations in Lowell, each of the weavers now tended four looms instead of three. In addition, the piece rate recently had been reduced by one cent.

Weekly wages then were about $2 for female operatives, and almost twice that for men doing the same work. Already there had been unsuccessful strikes organized by female workers in Lowell. But for the English immigrants taking the places of some of these former workers, conditions in Lowell looked comparatively good.

George Shipley found work at the Appleton Mills,[2] and settled his family into a house on Kirk Avenue in the center of town.

On September 22, 1851, Betty gave birth to Walter Shipley, their first American-born child. Walter died of convulsions a little more than a year later, on September 30, 1852.[3] The Shipleys had high hopes for life in the new country, but the beginnings were rough. Working at the cotton factory was, however, good for skilled workers such as George and Betty, because weavers were among the top-paid operatives.

The weaving process—from raw cotton to looms and woven into fabric—was a long and arduous task. Rev. Henry A. Miles described the process in *Lowell, As It Was, And As It Is*:

"The cotton purchased by agents at the South, and shipped to Boston, is brought to Lowell by the railroad, and deposited in storehouses ready for use. When wanted, it is wheeled by the yard hands to the carding-room, which is on the first floor of the mill. Here the bales are opened, and the cotton from different bales is well mixed together, in order to give the whole a more uniform appearance. It is then made to pass through a machine called the 'whipper,' by which it is beaten and thrown into a light state. Passing through another machine called the 'conical willow,' it comes out still more opened and cleansed, and is ready for the 'picker.' The picker rooms are two small buildings standing a few feet removed from the mill, and are made fire proof, in order to guard against ignition, which is liable to ensue from the great rapidity of the machinery. The cotton, laid on to a strip of cloth or leather called an 'apron,' is drawn into the picker when it is thoroughly opened and freed from lumps and dust, and then, passing through the 'lapper,' it comes out in sheets, nicely wound round a wooden cylinder. These laps are then taken to the card room, and are applied to the backs of cards. They go through two processes of carding, the first by the 'breaker,' after which the cotton passes through the 'lap-winder' or 'doubler,' by which it is wound again on the lap, and then through the 'finisher,' by which the carding process is completed. . . .

"The cotton is now taken by female operatives who carry it first through the 'drawing frame,' by which the fibres are laid in one direction, and are brought together in a rope-like form, then through the 'double speeder,' which twists this into a coarse 'roving,' and then through the 'stretcher,' which still further draws the roving out. In this stage it is packed in boxes, and by means of the

'elevator' it is taken up into the spinning room above. . . .
The spinning frames in Lowell are all 'throstles,' both
warp and filling. . . .

"On the speeders, throstles, warpers, and dressers,
there are clocks, which mark the quantity of work that is
done. The clocks are made to run one week, at the end of
which the overseer transfers the account to a board which
hangs in the room in the sight of all the operatives. From
this board the monthly wages of each operative are ascer-
tained. Dressing is paid higher than any other process,
because it demands peculiar skill and judgment. . . .

"The filling is now ready for the weaver; but the warp
undergoes yet further preparation in what is called the
'dressing room.' Here the yarn is warped off from the
spools upon section beams. These beams are then transferred to the dresser, who sizes, and brushes, and dries
the yarn. The yarn on eight of these beams is then transferred to a loom beam, the ends of the yarn being drawn
in through the harness and reed. This is done by hand,
and it is the first and only hand process in the manufacture of the fabric. . . .

"We now come to the weaving room, where the materials before prepared are put together in cloth. There
are two weaving rooms to each mill. In both rooms there
are from one hundred and thirty to one hundred and forty
weavers employed. Paid by the piece, their wages will
vary according to diligence and skill. . . . In the mills which
make the finer kinds of cloth, superior skill is required,
and wages will average somewhat more.

"When woven, the fabric is carried to the cloth
room. . . . The cloth is trimmed, measured, folded, and
recorded. It is then either baled, or delivered to the print
works."[4]

Certainly mill work is not for the idler. A typical work day
would begin with ringing bells to summon the operatives from
throughout the city. George would stand by his looms to see if
the warp yarn was correctly sized, brushed and dried, the ends
drawn in through the harness and reed. Then the waterwheel

would start to turn, and work would begin. George would get as much done as possible, so as to support his growing family. If no longer in the factory, Betty certainly was hard at work caring for the children.

During the next several years, the Shipleys moved often. They lived in various places for as little as six weeks or as "long" as 21 months. Although this made them difficult to track, it also demonstrated what many mill families were forced to tolerate to earn a living.

It was into this uncertain lifestyle that Mattie was born. Martha Jane "Mattie" Shipley was born September 18, 1856. Perhaps because Martha Platt was a stabilizing influence in Betty Shipley's life, Betty named her first American-born daughter after her sister. Mattie's birth is registered in Clinton, Worcester County, Massachusetts. She was born at Martha's house in Lowell, while her parents lived in Clinton. According to Martha Platt, the birth was attended by a professional nurse and midwife named Mary Hamilton.[5]

Births registered in Clinton, Massachusetts, 1856—including Martha Jane Shipley.

I was determined to locate Mattie's family in the state census, because it could clarify Betty's position in society. Did she still work as an operative or was she at home with her children? If she continued working, how did she manage? Was Millie helping to look after Mattie or were the older children working too? It was not uncommon for children to start working in the mills when they were as young as eight or nine years old.

While scanning the census for Lowell workers, I made an interesting observation: The number of female operatives at the mills far outnumbered the men. The Industrial Revolution was opening a new sphere of influence for women, contrary to the religious or popular sentiment of the day. Earning wages was creating a feeling of new independence and self esteem for women, though their wages remained much lower than men's.

The textile town of Clinton—about thirty-two miles southwest of Lowell on the Nashua River—was the home of gingham. The Lancaster Mill was the largest employer in Clinton, with 20,784 spindles and 550 looms.[6] When this mill first opened, just a few factory operatives lived in Clinton, so the operatives would have to be brought in from surrounding towns and housed in tenements. The owners of the Lancaster Mill said they would make the tenements as "attractive as possible in order that the workmen might find in them 'the pleasure of home,' and thus becoming attached to their surroundings, remain free from the desire of change so common among mill operatives."[7]

Apparently the Shipleys found Clinton "attractive" enough to stay for a few years. The last of George and Betty Shipley's children, Eliza Adelaide "Lida" Shipley, was born in Clinton on October 5, 1858. According to Martha Platt, however, the family moved from Clinton to Shirley when Lida was just six weeks old.[8] Lida's birth may have prompted the move, with George again looking for better employment or better living conditions for his growing family.

The mill town of Shirley is north of Clinton and southwest of Lowell. According to Lida's birth register, George still worked as a weaver after moving there and Betty apparently stayed home, as her child-rearing responsibilities continued to expand. If they hadn't already, the older children soon would prepare to enter the work force.

At this point in my research, I decided that I needed to head for Lowell. Certainly, sources there could be more beneficial for tracking the Shipleys. Besides, I wanted to experience Lowell and the mills, if possible. And most of all, I wanted to see where Mattie began her life. Economics obviously was part of the reason that the Shipleys moved around so much, but I felt sure there was something more going on.

Before going to Lowell, I desperately wanted to experience what it would have been like for Mattie and Ellery in Yellowstone during the last months of Mattie's life. So I convinced my sister, Georgia, and my husband, Paul, to snowmobile into the park to visit Mattie's grave.

We set off into Yellowstone on March 2, 1989—the 100th anniversary of the death of Mattie Shipley Culver.

It was snowing as we started our journey to Fountain Flat Drive, and it continued most of the day. A century ago, I thought, Mattie's and Ellery's isolation was almost complete; they could communicate, but transportation was limited to skis. They would have been amazed at the ease of travel the snow machines offered us today.

Approaching the area was difficult, even with our modern machinery, but we got as close as we could to the gravesite. Paul got off the snowmobile first and immediately sank to his waist. The snow was about five feet deep in Firehole Basin—as it likely was the winter that Mattie died.

We "swam" through white to find the gravestone. Just the very tips of the logs that protect the gravestone were visible. I don't know what I expected, but I really wanted to see the stone. We dug down five feet with our hands to clear the snow from it. We took lots of pictures, still and video. Someone recently told me they had been working in the park that winter and had snowmobiled to the same spot one day later, surprised to see the gravestone uncovered. Even in winter, people are drawn to Mattie's grave, to be sure that she is not forgotten on the anniversaries of her death.

After returning—tired, but safe and sound—to West Yellowstone, Paul and I focused on our upcoming trip to Lowell and other environs. I wanted to expand on Ellery Culver's early life, so the trip would continue to his birthplace in Vermont. And Cohoes, New York—Mattie's home for almost 20 years—was a must on the research trail as well.

As we headed across the country, we prepared ourselves for the congestion of Eastern cities. Lowell did not disappoint. There, we found narrow streets and red brick—red brick everywhere. I'll always think of that color and texture when I remember Lowell. I'll also think of the National Park Service when I think of Lowell—history is their expertise in this branch of the Park Service. And Lowell's center is set up to commemorate the city's industrial past. The Park Service has created a national historical park from the remains of the once-thriving textile industry that was so much a part of Mattie's early life. The rangers were thrilled to help with a project about a woman who was born in what now is a national park and who died in a national park.

We were treated to a personal tour of the area, with the added touch of a water-powered loom demonstration—before the display officially opened to the public. Then a local historian told me where I might find records of George Shipley's work.

The Shipleys had gone from Lowell to Clinton in search of better work, then from Clinton to Shirley. Why Shirley? Shirley was typical of other New England mill towns. George could choose from several factories there, all on the Catacumenaug River. Among them was the Fort Pond Mill, which was part of the bigger Shirley Cotton Mills, with 2,400 spindles. The Fredonia Mill, with 3,280 spindles and 68 looms, employed 56 operatives. It boasted "spacious boarding houses, and several smaller houses erected for the accommodation of married operatives."[9] The Lake Mill was smaller but two other larger manufactories always needed operatives.

The three-story Edgarton Manufactory, 114 feet long and 345 feet wide, housed 3,400 spindles and 80 looms and employed 50 operatives.

The Phoenix Mill, with its trademark bell tower, was the biggest manufactory, employing about 100 operatives; many were "foreigners" and more than half were female. This mill maintained 5,688 spindles, including 3,168 mule spindles and 2,520 ring and traveler spindles, plus 130 looms. Three blocks of two-story brick employee tenements were "designed for those operatives who have small families and wish to be housekeepers."[10] Another three-story brick boarding house accommodated operatives who did not have families. If George and Betty—and perhaps now William—chose to work for the Phoenix Mill, they likely lived in one of the tenements.

In classifying the operatives working for the Phoenix Mill, the elite of the city noted that "through careful supervision of the agents, the community connected with this manufactory have observed the moral propriety of life, though many of its members are of the lower class of foreigners, and possessed of little mental or educational culture."[11] This is the type of posturing that mill operatives, such as the Shipleys, had to endure.

Of course, the working class was guided by the same religious morals, the same code of community ethics, as the upper class. They lacked certain educational opportunities, but by no means were totally uneducated. They were striving for a better financial status and a better way of life; and some of the working class began to realize their goals. If this threatened the established elite, it was with good reason. These "foreigners" had skills for self-improvement that were perfected by years of hard work; they would not back away from their dreams.

The Shipleys essentially were no different. But Shirley was not the town of their dreams. Shortly after Lida was born, the family moved again.

I tracked the Shipleys to Newburgh, Orange County, New York via the 1860 federal census. My initial reaction was that Betty and Lida had died, because they were not listed with the rest of their family. Of course, I knew from George's military papers and from the Spokane census that this was not true. So where were Betty and Lida? Although I searched diligently, I could not find an answer.

George and William were working as operatives in 1860. Millie was not, nor was she attending school. She likely was taking care of household duties and looking after Mattie. Whatever happened to split the Shipley family apart between 1858 and 1860, we can only guess. And it would be a long time before Betty would be reunited with her children.

With this move, George took his family quite a distance from the Lowell area to find work. Newburgh in Orange County, New York was not the type of textile town to which they were accustomed. Although cotton manufacturing had been going on in Newburgh since at least 1844, and the Hudson River Woolen Mills offered job opportunities in weaving, there appeared to be more work in finished products in the garment industry there. Whatever work George and William had in Newburgh, it didn't hold the family for long. Yet another move was in store for the Shipleys—this time to the mill town of Cohoes, New York.

---

[1] Robert O'Brien with Richard D. Brown, *The Encyclopedia of New England* (New York, New York and Oxford, England: Facts On File Publications), p. 277.

[2] 1853 Lowell, Massachusetts City Directory.

[3] Death Register, Lowell, Massachusetts—1852.

[4] Rev. Henry A. Miles, *Lowell, As It Was, And As It Is* (Lowell: Nathaniel L. Dayton, Merrill & Heywood, 1846), pp. 76-84.

[5] Petition for pension, military papers of George Shipley.

[6] Andrew E. Ford, *History of the Origin of the Town of Clinton, Massachusetts* (Clinton: Press of W.J. Coulter, 1896), p. 333.

[7] Ibid. p. 226.

[8] Petition for pension, military papers of George Shipley.

[9] Seth Chandler, *History of the Town of Shirley* (Shirley, Massachusetts: Seth Chandler 1883), p. 49.

[10] Ibid. p. 50.

[11] Ibid. p. 51.

Chapter 3

Growing Up in Cohoes

here was good reason that the Shipley family lived in Cohoes, New York longer than in any other single location. From 1855 to 1860, its business sector was flourishing; 3,728 operatives were employed in its factories by 1860. Prospects looked good for George and William, and there would be opportunities for Millie and Mattie as well.

Industrial development in Cohoes began in 1811, when the power of the Mohawk River and Cohoes Falls was ideal for mills. But by the 1860s, when the Shipley family moved to Cohoes, the original force

An early view of the once-powerful Cohoes Falls. Today, only a trickle runs over the massive rock ledge.

and beauty of the falls was tamed by dams and mill races. Today, just a small trickle runs over a massive rock ledge, and power lines and fences mar even that sight.

Red brick, narrow streets, and lines of frame houses offer impressions of the great factory town that Cohoes must have been. But prodigious building complexes that once housed hundreds of looms—now textile factory outlets and other various businesses—remind us how fragile our occupations are, especially those dependent upon changing industry and technology.

Perhaps George Shipley could foresee the eventual southern movement of the factories; perhaps he wanted more from his new country. In the end, opportunity would emerge from a field of employment that he never may have contemplated.

In the spring of 1861, at the start of the Civil War, Cohoes began to enroll men for its local brigades. The town raised funds to support volunteers' families. In the beginning, many young men were lured to other communities, even other states, because of the high bounties offered to enlistees. Quotas had to be filled in Cohoes, so it also increased the amount offered for enlistment. By September,1862, the Cohoes town bounty was $100.

William Shannon opened a recruiting office in July, 1862, and George Shipley was one of sixty men who enlisted. Shipley was forty years old when he signed up on July 5. He is described as 5-feet-5-inches tall, with grey eyes and dark hair. William Shipley assumed the role of head of the household, as George joined Company I, 7th New York Volunteer Artillery, on August 18, 1862. This was the last time that William, Millie, and five-year-old Mattie would see their father. His youngest daughter, Lida, would never know him.

It seems that eighteen-year-old William would have been the more likely candidate for the Army. Was George protecting his son's future? Was some of the bounty money earmarked to support his wife and daughter back in Lowell? George received a $25 advance bounty when he enlisted; it may have only been about a month's wages at the time but it certainly would help. And more money would come in as he served.

As the war continued, the local paper followed the military activity of its soldiers. Shared letters were published by permission. The new Ladies Aid Society collected donations from businessmen and held concerts and festivals for the Soldiers' Relief Fund. I can imagine Millie joining its ranks to do what she could to support her father, so far away.

When some of the regiments that enlisted in 1861 began to return in 1863, the Shipley family hoped to welcome their father home soon, too. The greeting parties were not all joyous, though, as the local paper, the *Cataract*, noted with the return of the 10th Regiment on September 5, 1863:

> "The anticipated joy with which the return of the 10th Reg't was to be welcomed was sadly marred when they appeared on Tuesday, by their wretched condition. Worn out, decimated by battles and fevers, sick and dying, tottering feebly or borne by others to their homes, it was almost impossible to believe that the splendid regiment which left Albany nine months ago over 1,000 strong had indeed returned. Not over 250 men could be numbered who were in the enjoyment of even moderate health."

Still, the Shipley children held tight to hopes for the safe return of their father. But it was not to be. In May, 1864, George was wounded in the hip by a rifle ball. He received medical treatment, but by July 6, was admitted to the first division hospital with remittent fever. On July 9, he was transferred to the Depot Field Hospital, 2nd A.C. City Point, Virginia. He was failing quickly, so on July 11, George was admitted to the Hospital Steamer Atlantic. But the next day, while en route to New York, he died. George was buried on July 14, 1864 in Cyprus Hill Cemetery, Long Island, New York. His children would have to make their own way in the world.

Plunging earnestly into work would help William and Millie through the emotionally draining first months of grief. But Mattie, who was not yet working, probably yearned for the hustle and bustle of the mills, to help pass the hours and days of loneliness.

The war continued, but spring brought news of Union victories. Richmond fell and Lee surrendered. Cohoes was still in the midst of celebration when news of Lincoln's assassination was announced. On April 25, 1865, Lincoln lay in state at the capitol in Albany. Hundreds from Cohoes traveled there to pay their last respects. On the day of the funeral, businesses suspended work.

The rest of the spring and early summer seemed calm compared to the excitement that the end of the war brought. Cohoes' July 4 celebration was unusually large in 1865. The day was clear and pleasant and no doubt heightened the sorrow of separation for William, Millie and Mattie. But they certainly felt pride when the day began with the ringing of bells and the procession lead by Company I, 7th Artillery, New York Volunteers. If only George was among them.

At the end of the war, when many men were returning to their families, Mattie and her siblings were living in the household of the George Bray family. A son, Joseph Bray, served in the same company with George Shipley and undoubtedly told stories about him that helped make the lonely times easier.

Many of the men in George Shipley's company had been factory operatives before the war and now returned to their work. One of those men was William Alston. But William's son, David, who had joined the Army from an Ohio company, stayed in Cohoes only briefly before beginning a westward trek to find his fortune. It was during his short stay in Cohoes that Millie Shipley met David and sealed some sort of pledge with him.

The Shipley children moved quickly into skilled positions in the factories. By 1865, William was a knitter and Millie was a weaver, but eight-year-old Mattie had not yet started working as an operative. The census enumeration of the Bray household indicated a housekeeper, Hannah Bailey, so Mattie did have someone to supervise her—and perhaps even offer motherly advice.

Fortunately, because William and Millie were skilled workers, Mattie did not have to start working as young as her brother and sister had. Even by 1870, when fourteen-year-old Mattie no longer was in school, the combined family income allowed her to stay home and housekeep for her siblings—no small job in itself. Still living under the same roof as George Bray, (he had remarried to a woman named Margaret Mather, and she had brought her six children to the household), Mattie had plenty of company and advice.

Some of Mattie's early memories of Cohoes would include the Harmony Company's excavation of the remains of a huge mastadon beneath Cohoes and the torn-up streets and confusion connected to the construction of the line of Cohoes and Troy Horse Rail Road Company—a horse-drawn street railway. At first, merchants opposed construction of the railway because they believed their trade would suffer and that property values along the line would decrease. Eventually, however, opposition faded as people realized the growth it would bring to their town; transportation in the village was easily attainable now, and connecting to other cities and towns was convenient. It wasn't long before the railway superseded all other forms of travel, and an additional horse railroad was built. Still, Mattie had no idea how important the railroad would be to her future.

Mattie soon had to leave her housekeeping duties at home to enter the work force. She likely started in one of the unskilled, lower-paying positions before moving into the family tradition of weaving. Mattie might have thought that her life was frenetic up until now, but the rest of her years would prove even more so.

The year of 1873 was especially full of change. On May 17, William married Esther Electa Bottum, leaving Millie and Mattie to fend for themselves. Electa was the daughter of Elijah and Minerva Bottum. Elijah was a teamster in Cohoes, and most of the Bottum children became factory operatives when they finished school. Electa worked in the cotton mills, probably alongside the Shipley sisters. William was twenty-eight and Electa was twenty-four when they married.

Millie and Mattie now spread their wings and flew into young womanhood away from the watchful eye of their older brother. And they flew right into the winds of change. The failure of Jay Cooke and Company banking house in September, 1873 set off a financial panic in the country, arousing particular fear in the textile-manufacturing companies in Cohoes. The first repercussions struck in October. The mills cut wages and reduced working hours. Harmony Mills began the first shutdown on October 25, and others would follow. Workers feared that the mills would not reopen again until spring.

The *Cataract* tried to uphold the spirit of the community:

"There is as yet nothing very discouraging in the prospects before us, and if all will take courage and push ahead as far as circumstances will allow, everything will come out right, and we shall see a far more favorable winter's business than has been predicted."

The stoppage lasted just two weeks, but when the mills reopened, there were two fewer woolen mills operating. Seven of the mills ran full time and the rest ran half and three-quarter time. When Harmony Mills reopened on November 24, wages were reduced an average of 12 percent. Depression and disillusionment—though no more closures—continued until 1878.

Nationwide, the textile industry was just one of many businesses affected by the bank failure. Jay Cooke and Company also had financed construction of the Northern Pacific Railroad. With the 1873 collapse, the company halted progress of the railroad across the Dakota Territory at Bismarck. Little did Millie and Mattie know that those now-unfinished tracks one day would guide them toward a new phase of their lives.

But for now, the focus for the Shipley sisters was a new home in Cohoes. From the frame house in which they lived with the George Bray family, Millie and Mattie moved to the household of the Bold family, in one of the many brick tenements that the mills operated. Susan Bold had two sons and a daughter, all working as operatives. Having a woman instead of a man as head of the household would provide a role model for the Shipley sisters as they took full control of their own lives and futures.

Of course, much of their lives already was controlled by others, especially at work. Mattie and Millie worked twelve hours a day, and women in the factories were making about $1 a day, or $6 a week. Men doing the same job made about $1.50 a day. This was a slight improvement for women from the days when George Shipley moved his family to Lowell.

Considering the workings of the looms, it is astounding that Mattie and Millie endured their work for as long as they did. The noise is deafening; you can't hear anything above the rhythm of the waterwheel and belts, gears and looms. The odors are overpowering, emanating from the machinery grease and the oil on the wooden floors to keep the yarn's lint down. Were they even aware of what they were breathing? What did they think of the illness called "white lung," which was so common among their co-workers? Was "The Great Lung Remedy, Masta's Indian Pulmonic Balsam, for the cure of coughs, colds, hoarseness, sore throats, bronchitis, catarrh, influenza, croup, whooping cough, asthma, consumption, and all other affections of the lungs and chest," going to work for them?[1]

The operatives used the remedy—manufactured in Lowell—but continued to work. They didn't have the economic advantages of the middle and upper classes; the opportunity to become an "invalid" did not apply to them.[2] In her book, *Living in the Shadow of Death, Tuberculosis and the Social Experience of Illness in American History,* Sheila M. Rothman writes: "Invalids were allowed to modify, or in extreme cases, to avoid the obligation to earn an income or to fulfill duties of wife and mother." But this choice was not available for the mill operative. Until 1882, consumption was not believed to be a communicable disease, at least not in the United States. People had no idea how easily the disease was spread. Infected operatives coughed, and airborne lint carried tubercle bacilli from person to person. One of every eight deaths was attributed to consumption, but this was hardly the only life-threatening situation the operatives faced. Fire was a constant threat, and precautions were few. Operatives at various mills often were killed or injured in factory fires and accidents.

Operatives used song as a release from the worries of mill life, as illustrated by the "Song of the Spinners":

> The day is o'er, nor longer we toil and spin;
> For evening's hush withdraws from the daily din.
> And now we sing, with gladsome hearts,
> The theme of the spinner's song,
> That labor to leisure a zest imparts,
> Unknown to the idle throng.
>
> We spin all day, and then, in the time for rest,
> Sweet peace is found, a joyous and welcome guest.
> Despite of toil we all agree,
> Or out of the Mills, or in,
> Dependent on others we ne'er will be,
> So long as we're able to spin.[3]

Work, religion and play helped Mattie survive her years in Cohoes. Her twelve free hours a day had to be split between sleep, household duties, religious obligations, and recreational activities.

Recreation was an important part of Mattie's life, and she had a choice of amusements in Cohoes. Some of the mills established singing evenings, which often drew as many as 500 people. Then there were the free velocipede exhibitions. A walk to Cohoes Falls offered a powerfully beautiful sight during spring runoff, the only time of the year that the falls were as full as they were before the mills took the power for themselves. Visiting friends was important in a time when communication was still done in person. And, as early as 1863, Cohoes had a skating association; a skating park was established in 1865. "Who put out the light on the rink March 1st?" Alice Mather asks Mattie in a February 29, 1879 entry in Mattie's autograph book.

Public lectures, books and magazines also were leisurely outlets. It was becoming common for women to speak publicly about women's rights, suffrage, the labor movement and temperance. New ideas, theories, and discoveries abounded. Something new was happening all the time: The incandescent lamp and Thomas Edison were the talk; President Grant signed a law that created a national park called Yellowstone; Alexander Graham Bell patented the telephone; and the Sioux battled United States Troops at Little Big Horn in Montana Territory.

As 1875 came to a close, the village of Cohoes readied itself for the country's centennial celebration. The festivities began in the evening on December 31 and continued until about 3 a.m. of the new year. Nineteen years old and ready for the gala, Mattie joined her family, neighbors and co-workers to enjoy the fireworks, noise and demonstrations of the celebration:

> "The celebration of the Centennial New Year in Cohoes was begun by the parade of the Lafayette Guards shortly before the ringing of the bells at midnight. Remsen street was thronged with people, whose patriotism added to the spirit with which the new year is always welcomed, caused a general turn out and demonstration. Huge bonfires were lighted, red and blue fire burned, cannon thundered, rockets and roman candles were fired and numerous buildings along the route illuminated. The bells of the city churches and factories clanged forth a thousand welcomes in brazen tones to

the Centennial New Year, and even the steam whistles on the mills and Adams Steamer (a local steam fire engine) did duty on the occasion."[4]

All these events of the 1870s would affect Mattie more personally than she could imagine. For the time being, though, she would experience them with curiosity and awe while continuing one day at a time.

Mattie and Millie were lovingly reunited with their younger sister, Lida, when she came to live in Cohoes by 1878. What caused Lida to join her sisters is only speculation. Their mother, Betty, remained in Lowell, close to her own sister, Martha Platt. But it was only a matter of time before Betty would share company with her daughters again.

---

[1] Advertisement for "Masta's Indian Pulmonic Balsam," from the 1859 Lowell, Massachusetts City Directory.

[2] "For most of the nineteenth century men and women with chronic and debilitating respiratory ailments, carrying the harbingers of consumption or already afflicted with the disease, defined themselves and were defined by others as invalids." Sheila M. Rothman, *Living in the Shadow of Death, Tuberculosis and the Social Experience of Illness in American History* (New York, New York: Basic Books, 1994), p. 22.

[3] "Song of the Spinners," *The Lowell Offering*, December, 1840, p. 63.

[4] *Cohoes Daily News*, 2 January 1876.

Chapter 4

Signs of the Times

"The individual is frequently called upon for his or her auto-graph. In complying, it is customary to couple with the same a sentiment, signing the name beneath. If the matter written is original, be it long or short, it is usually more highly valued."
Hill's Manual of Social and Business Forms[1]

Mattie Jane Shipley's autograph book, along with a set of the family's napkin rings with the inscriptions "Mother," "Mattie," and "Theda."

In Mattie's time, trading autographs was a common way to share with friends, similar to the way students exchange class photographs today. Mattie's autograph book was the single most important item that Edwin Jelsing sent. Without that, it would have been more difficult to locate Mattie, and I certainly would not have been able to identify her co-workers, friends and relatives.

The people to whom you are about to be introduced are Mattie's friends. They help define Mattie because she left no written words of her own, other than her signature. All of these words are to her and about her. Mattie received the book on December 25, 1878 "from a friend," and added new autographs regularly until 1883.

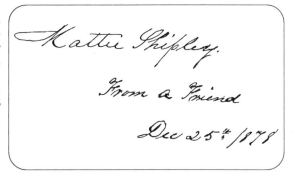

Because the fountain pen was not invented until 1884, all of the autographs in Mattie's book used pens dipped in ink. This signature is on the first page of the book.

Because Mattie's brother, William, was the head of the household until 1873, it was his job to see that his younger siblings were cared for and had religious instruction. This is evident in the autograph he wrote to Mattie on March 8, 1879 (original spelling retained):

Mattie,
Where ever you may be, may peace and contentment be your lot, may health and prosperity be your portion, and may you never witness or exeriance in your household, sickness, sorrow, pain or distress. May friendship encircle you like ivy. May every honest endeavor be crowned with success. May you ever live happy and in harmony with God's laws, and may your life be long and full of usefullness, and may blessings continually increase. And at the end of life's journey may you be able to look back and not find one footstep you would wish to retrace, nor one act you wish had not been performed. And when the lamp of life is about to expire may there not be one rude blast to hasten its expiration and, in the morning of the reserection may you be found with those on God's right hand is the wish of your brother.

William S. Shipley

William's concern for Mattie's well-being is evident through-out his writing. He was vestryman and Sunday School superin-tendent for St. John's Episcopal Church and apparently tried to surround Mattie with people who would instill in her a founda-tion of faith as part of her daily life.

Although we can assume that church was important in Mattie's life, we must question how big a role it played. She and Ellery Culver were married in church, but it is unclear whether or not they were members. There is no record of a baptism for their daughter, Theda, and Mattie never was baptized either, as noted by Millie in her mother's application for pension: "I was the oldest daughter of Elizabeth, and know that neither of my sisters were ever baptized."

The Brays, with whom the Shipleys lived for many years af-ter their father's death, also were influential in Mattie's life. George Bray gave Mattie some words of strength and encour-agement in his autograph on January 13, 1881:

> To Mattie
> > Stand up for the cold-water fight
> > gainst doctor and lawyer and priest
> > Stand up and do battle for right
> > gainst foes from the west or the east
> > gainst foes from the north or the south
> > gainst foes from above or beneath
> > Speak out, every man with a mouth
> > the watchword of "freedom or death"

George Bray asked Mattie to speak her mind and stand her ground. His sentiments are much like the ones of those trying to organize better working conditions for the factory employees. Could Mattie have been involved in the early labor movement? Or per-haps George was referring to some activity in the women's-rights movement, where "foes" were in every corner.

The next words came from authority figures who sought to show Mattie the power of religion. R.H. Vaughan was a second-hand dealer whose children and stepchildern were factory op-eratives. The family lived in West Troy. Perhaps Mattie knew him through church or from associating with his daughters, who were working "at collars." (One of the major industries in Troy, New York was making and laundering collars, around which an early women's trade union formed.)

Vaughan, a sec-ondhand dealer whose family lived in West Troy, New York, probably knew Mattie through church or her ac-quaintance with his daughters.

> Religion should be th chief concern
> Of mortals here below
>
> R H Vaughan
>
> Feb 26 th /79

> To Mattie   As the Sun in great splendor sheds its rays over all the universe, so may God in His great love for all His children, shed His divine rays over thy pathway. And if the dark house which perchance may come to thee in thy pilgrimage; let that influence most divine make thee a willing captive unto Him who wipes all tears away binds up the broken heart and heals us in the eternal day.
>
> Feb 8th 1880   Your friend J.H.W.

In this autograph, signed "Your friend F.H.W." in February, 1880, the theme obvi-ously was in-tended to guide Mattie down the correct path on her "pilgrimage."

Robert Mac-Kinnon, a single man just a few years older than Mattie, was an operative in a woolen mill. He may have worked with her brother, William, at the Globe Mill.

> To Mattie.
>
> When the love of Christ fills the heart there is happiness. It seems as if Jesus like a master musician, strikes the chords of the soul, and fills it with the sweetest melodies. That no chord will ever be touched but that will bring forth notes of rejoicing to you here, and, in the harmonies of eternity is the earnest wish of your friend   Robert Mac Kinnon
>
> Cohoes Mar. 28th 1879

"A noble deed is a step toward God."

With loving wishes,
Marianna Gay

Germantown, Dec. 27, '78

Marianna Gay signed this autograph from Germantown, a small town south of Cohoes, N.Y., in Columbia County.

The handwriting from this autograph of E.S. Bell matches that of the person who presented the book to Mattie.

"The flower of youth never appears more beautiful than when it bends to the Son of Righteousness"

Truly Your friend
E. S. Bell

A Bell family lived in the same area of Cohoes as the Shipleys, and the head of that household was Edward. He was a teamster and had a daughter, Emma, who worked in the cotton mill. One of the Bells likely gave Mattie the autograph book.

Mattie's friends seemed to be from her work, her neighborhood and probably her church. As many men as women signed her book, and the following selections represent the humor in her life.

Several of the themes touched on in the autographs deal with marriage, which probably was on the minds of many young women and men of the day. Their lives were ripe for change. They were starting to look forward from the depression of 1873-1878 and beginning to see renewed hope in the world around them.

In sharp contrast to the serious tone of brother William's entry, sister-in-law Electa Bottum Shipley keeps the sentiment short and funny.

To Mattie

I wish you a husband kind and true
Fond of himself but fonder of you.
Electa E. Shipley.
Cohoes.
Aug 27th 1879.   N.Y.

Mattie

I hope the one you marry with bliss will fill your cup
& he will be one of those men to who you can look up

J. A. Syke

Philada Jan 7. 1880

This interesting autograph is signed from "Philada." Mattie seems to have spent a significant amount of time in Philadelphia during 1880.

It doesn't seem like Mattie went to Philadelphia just to visit. From late November, 1879 until June, 1880, several autographs were entered by people who I was unable to track to Cohoes or nearby towns. There were, in fact, no Cohoes entries again until December, 1880. Some of the autographs signed during this period were identified with "Frankford," and some did not list a place at all. While trying to find J.A. Syke in Philadelphia, Pennsylvania, I discovered that Frankford had been a town just outside of Philadelphia and, by 1880, was encompassed by Ward 23 of the city. Frankford's main industry was cotton manufacturing.

In records of Philadelphia's Ward 23, I located at least two people who could have been the author of the J.A. Syke autograph. The family of Edward and Anna Lee was there, too. Their three youngest daughters—Lide, a cotton weaver; Satie, who was at home; and Amanda, a student—all signed Mattie's book.

Lide wrote:
> Remember me in the morning
> And when only half awake
> Remember me on your wedding day
> And send me a piece of cake.

Satie penned:
> I thought—I thought—I thought in vain,
> At last I thought I would write my name.

And 14-year-old Amanda added:
> When you are old, and cannot see,
> Put on your specks and think of me.

I was certain I would find traces of Mattie and her sisters in Philadelphia. The Lee sisters were counted in the 1880 census on June 11 and signed Mattie's book on June 19. The Shipley sisters were not in Ward 23 of Philadelphia; apparently they didn't live as close to the Lees as I first imagined. But this did indicate that Mattie—perhaps in search of work or simply a change of environment—traveled some and was ready to alter her life if necessary.

Lizzie E. Creighton, Katie Bacon, F.R. Bacon, and Anna Bryer were other friends who signed Mattie's autograph book during her Philadelphia sojourn.

Mattie was back in Cohoes by the end of 1880, perhaps to share the holidays with William and Electa. She continued to add autographs to her book:

Recognize the 'Bold' surname from the family with whom Mattie and Millie lived after William married. You can almost hear the fun they shared in the household.

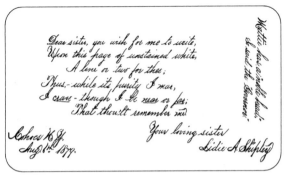

Sister Lida's auto-
graph is composed
carefully. Even
her addition at the
side is beautifully
penned. A lot can
be read into this
addition; she could
be referring to
Mattie's qualities or
her ideals.

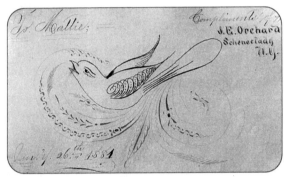

James Orchard
must have been
special to Mattie.
He signed the
book twice, mak-
ing artistic im-
pact. This draw-
ing is like one in
Hill's Manual of
Social & Business
Forms.

Mattie's book includes five autographs from the Orchard family, two of which are signed at Schenectady, New York. Deborah
Orchard, Mattie's close friend, probably was the connection to the
rest of the family, which was scattered between the two cities.

Some of the sentiments of the autographs suggest only ac-
quaintanceship, while others appear rather personal. An interesting contrast also emerges. While most of William's in-laws
signed the book, not one member of the Alston family, Millie's
soon-to-be in-laws, signed. Because Millie was not yet actually
married to David Alston at the time Mattie's book was circulat-
ing, there simply may not have been a connection with the family.

Mattie's close circle of friends, who refer to each other as "The
Hens," certainly stamped their distinctive mark on the pages of
the autograph book. Each of them had a number, some of them
a "Port Name," and most of them put an applique or two on the
page. Some included a phrase that seemed to hold meaning just

between the two women. All of them were operatives; all of them were women; and all of them lived close to each other. There were at least ten "Hens," counting Mattie.

Although "Hen" and other females of the animal kingdom traditionally have been derogatory terms for women, some history surrounding the word "Hen" seems to fit the situation of the mill workers here. Women's-rights proponents apparently were somewhat amusing to the general population and frequently were referred to as "hens attempting to crow." The press referred to meetings or conventions of these people as "hen conventions." Mattie and her friends might well be referring to themselves as "Hens" because of their support for the women's-rights movement. Certainly there is pride here as they number themselves among the "Hens":

Ellenor Hill had the distinction of being "Hen No.1" & "Port Schulyer." Maybe she was born there or had worked there. She and the next two women signed the book on a Monday, a work day.

"Hen No. 2," Anna Van Leuven, was a woolen weaver and also "Port Misery." She had an interesting sense of humor for one with such a dismal nickname.

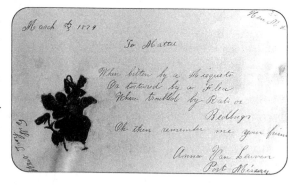

Also a woolen weaver, Ellenor McLaren, "No. 3 of the Hens," found comfort in her friends' company and pork pies.

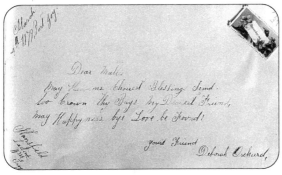

"Port Joy" and "No. 4 of Hens," Deborah Orchard, boarded with Ellenor (Hen No. 1) Hill's family. Also a woolen weaver, she was the eldest of the clutch, at 24, in 1879.

Youngest of the "Hens," Marion Muir, "Hen No. 9," was one of four members of the Muir family who signed Mattie's autograph book.

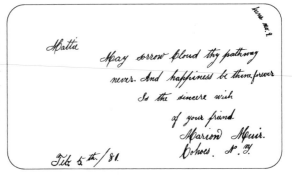

While none of the autographs are specific about whether or not Mattie had plans to leave Cohoes, perhaps we can read between the lines in some of them. Looking at her siblings' words (except for Millie, who does not have an entry in the book), you might deduce that Mattie was planning a trip. Assuming it would take a few years to save enough money for a train ticket, William's 1879 entry may refer to the possibility that Mattie could be somewhere other than Cohoes. "Where ever you may be. . ."

Lida emphasizes words in her entry by underlining them. "I <u>crave</u>—though I be <u>near</u> or <u>far</u>. . . ." Here again, Lida may have been referring to travel plans Mattie might have had. It also is interesting that there is no autograph from Millie. Maybe Mattie was planning to be with Millie, and so felt no need to have a remembrance of her in the autograph book.

Anna Breyer might have been one of a select few with whom Mattie shared her plans to leave Cohoes:

> Remember me when far away,
> When every thing is bright and gay,
> And let the name of Anna be;
> Impressed upon your memory.

Lizzie Creighton also might have known Mattie's plans. She signed the autograph book twice. In one, she emphasized her words, "When all the world <u>your secrets know</u>. . ." and begins another by writing:

> When in distant lands we roam
> And far from friends and far from home.
> And when these simple lines you see,
> Think of the one who thinks of thee.

Perhaps more telling in its simple way is one of the last autographs of the book. Kate McLean writes from New York:

> Should "Auld acquaintance be forgot!"

May 15, 1881 is the date on the second-to-last autograph in the book, and it is still from New York. The last autograph is dated Billings, (Montana), April 17, 1883. The two years between these last autographs turned out to be the most difficult time period for which to document Mattie's movements. They also were very eventful years for Mattie and embodied much personal change for her. It is from this point that Mattie's strong personality begins to emerge and that the picture of an adventurous woman begins to take form.

---

[1] Thomas E. Hill, *Hill's Manual of Social and Business Forms,* (Chicago: Moses Warren & Co., 1880), p. 138.

Chapter 5

Heading West

I desperately wanted to find out just how Mattie made the move from Cohoes to Montana Territory and why. These things I knew: Mattie eventually married Ellery Culver in Billings, Montana, but she previously had been married to a Mr. Gillett; Millie Shipley Alston's first two children were born in Montana; and Mattie and Ellery's child, Theda, was born in Billings. Articles and columns in Billings newspapers, plus information from David Alston's military-pension history helped pinpoint the area of Montana, then in Custer County, called Pease Bottom. From these bits and pieces of information emerged the story of Mattie's journey and her new life in Montana.

Pease Bottom gets its name from Fort Pease, the last of a succession of stockades, near the mouth of the Bighorn River. An expedition led by Major Fellow B. Pease built Fort Pease in 1875. Major Pease was known for his lifelong friendship with the Indians, but the government already was making plans to "control" the Sioux. Fort Pease was built as a defense and a trading post. Incessant Indian raids made the fort difficult to protect and, after the Battle at Little Big Horn, it was abandoned. Fort Pease later was burned and, over time, was washed into the river.

The first of the forts in and around the area was built in 1807, when Manuel Lisa established a trading post, known by several names—Lisa's Fort, Fort Manuel, and Fort Raymon. In 1811, the fort was abandoned. Ten years later, the Missouri Fur Company, which Manuel Lisa helped form, built a post at the same location and named it Fort Benton (not to be confused with the Fort Benton established in Chouteau County in 1850.) It too, soon was abandoned. William Henry Ashley and Andrew Henry, founders of the Rocky Mountain Fur Company, tried again in 1822 with the short-lived Fort Henry. Fort Cass (also on some maps as Fort Tullock) was built in 1832 by Samuel Tullock of the American Fur Company. After the Battle of Little Big Horn, Pease Bottom was ripe for settlement. The Northern Pacific Railroad was getting back on track, and immigration West was as attractive as ever.

The Northern Pacific was chartered in 1864, the year that George Shipley died. The new railroad would travel an ambitious route from Lake Superior to Puget Sound, following portions of the Lewis and Clark trail. Congress granted the Northern Pacific title to all odd-numbered sections of land within ten miles of each side of the railroad line in the states and all odd-numbered sections of land within twenty miles each side of the railroad line in the territories. That garnered the railroad company between 47 million and 60 million acres of land!

Very few of the Northern Pacific land holdings sold in the Pacific district (from the Rocky Mountains to the Pacific Coast) before 1874. But with the failure of Jay Cooke and Company, Northern Pacific land became valuable. Investors and settlers exchanged their almost-worthless bonds for the desirable land. In 1874, land sales tripled and, in 1875, they were eight times higher still; in April, 1875, Northern Pacific went into receivership.

Frederick Billings, who later would become president of Northern Pacific, devised a plan for reorganization, which was completed by September, 1875. Road construction resumed in 1877, at which time the company began to encourage new settlement:

"Millions and millions of acres of Northern Pacific Railroad LANDS FOR SALE at the lowest prices ever offered by any railroad company, ranging chiefly from $2.60 to $4.00 per acre, for the best wheat lands, best farming lands, best grazing lands in the world. These extremely productive lands stretch out for 50 miles on each side of the Northern Pacific Railroad, and extend from the Great Lakes to the Pacific Ocean. An equal amount of government lands, lying in alternate sections with the Railroad lands, and FREE TO ALL, are open for settlement under the homestead, pre-emption, tree-culture laws, all through Minnesota, Dakota, Montana, Idaho, Washington and Oregon, the great new Northern Pacific Country!"[1]

How could someone looking for a new start have resisted such promises? Moving West was a logical choice for an ambitious young man discontented with his role in life. The kind of work or life that David Alston began searching for is lost to us, but the lure of land in the West likely sparked his imagination, as he left Cohoes just a few years after returning to the mills following his miliary service.

With his younger brother, Joseph, David began the search for land to settle. What he knew about farming or ranching would have been extremely limited because he and his parents had been city people, engaged in the world of the industrial revolution.

If David Alston could not afford to buy land from the Northern Pacific Railroad, certainly he could take advantage of one of the government programs. The homestead law, enacted January 1, 1863, allowed 160 acres to settlers. Military land grants had five-year homestead requirements. How could David go wrong?

David's military pension records reveal that he lived in Etchetah, Custer County, Montana Territory. The 1880 Montana census indicated that he and his brother, Joseph, were "farming" on Froze to Death Creek in Pease Bottom. Old maps of the area locate Etchetah in the bottomland along the Yellowstone River, appropriately named Pease Bottom. Froze to Death Creek flows into the Yellowstone River east of the confluence of the Bighorn River and the Yellowstone. Pease Bottom is north of Custer's Battle Ground and the Crow Indian Reservation, on the north bank of the Yellowstone River.

By the time David and his brother arrived in Pease Bottom, two forts—Custer and Keogh—had been established in Custer County to protect the settlers and subjugate the Indians, dissenting because of the destruction of their food source, the bison. Fort Custer was a cavalry post at the junction of the Bighorn and the Little Bighorn rivers, and Fort Keogh, built in 1877, was where modern-day Miles City, Montana is located.

When David started farming on Froze to Death Creek, a few settlers already were established. John C. Guy and his son, Robert, had been working 160 acres along the Yellowstone River since the fall of 1876. John Guy's wife, Amanda Green Guy, joined them in 1878. The Guys were old hands at frontier life, having spent time in Alder Gulch, Montana. They also had run a hotel in Bozeman called the Guy House—the place to stay while establishing a new home in the city.

Near his ranch in the southwestern Pease Bottom valley, John Guy established the post office of Etchetah. According to local residents of the area today, Etchetah means "horse" in Crow. The Crows were considered wealthy because of their huge horse herds and commerce in horses to other tribes. By the time David Alston arrived, Etchetah boasted a store, stage station, steamboat landing, wood yard and saloon.

Among other settlers the Alstons would call neighbors were the Joe Allen family, William and Gavin Nouat, Wiley King, John Strauss, Andrew Lindsay, the Joseph and Catherine Isaac family, the W.B.S. and Lucinda Higgins family and the family of Robert Grierson. In a letter to his brother, Robert Grierson describes Pease Bottom:

> "I considered it good land though not black and the amount of bottom land is small compared with the big extent of grassland around. This part of Montana grows grain without irrigation. This country is on the sandstone and coal formation—no gold on it. As to objections— the insects are pretty bad and next to that horse stealing by the straggling Indians is too common. I most decidedly think this is the best of the United States to go to— and now (March) is the proper time as far as climate affects the production of corn, watermelons, pumpkins and such like. It is not a smooth, bare plain but river bottoms for farming sheltered with grassy hills that afford lots of free pasturage for stock. And another advantage is the

construction of the Northern Pacific Railroad. Another advantage, this is the center of grazing grounds of the great buffalo."[2]

It's no wonder that the Alston brothers chose this spot. The early years of settlement in Pease Bottom were wet ones, and growing crops was easy. The farmers grew and sold oats to forts Custer and Keogh. With the prospect of continued prosperity, David decided he was ready for Millie to join him.

In Mattie's autograph book, entries from New York end one month before Millie and David's marriage in Bismarck, Dakota Territory. There are no witnesses listed on that marriage record to indicate that Mattie was at the wedding, but because her documented life begins again in Pease Bottom, presumably she, and perhaps even Lida, accompanied Millie to Montana. While David was preparing their future home, Millie, Mattie and Lida would be preparing for the journey west.

I wondered how much the Shipley sisters communicated with their mother during this transition. I was trying to tie up loose ends in the "East" by doing a little more research about Martha Platt and her family when, to my surprise, I spotted Betty Shipley's name in the 1880 Lowell census; at that time, she was living in Martha's household at 12 Dodge Street. I finally had located Mattie's mother!

By 1880, Martha Platt was widowed, and one of her daughters, Claudine, was living with her and working at a print works. Betty Shipley now was a nurse. Because Lida already had moved to Cohoes by then, Betty's life probably was a little easier, and perhaps a little lonelier too. But that was 1880. What did Betty Shipley think of her daughters' plans to go West one year later?

As I began to research Pease Bottom, an exciting package arrived for me from Spokane. Some of its contents led me to believe that Betty Shipley had not let her daughters slip away from her altogether. The package was from Heidi Jelsing, Edwin Jelsing's granddaughter. He had died, and she was going through his belongings. She came across my original correspondence to him and was sending along more things that she determined were from the previous owners. Some of the things she sent included Mattie's, Theda's and Betty Shipley's inscribed silver napkin rings; I was thrilled to be holding another of Mattie's personal belongings! I also received some diaries that Grace Alston Hedrick kept during the years encompassing World War II, plus a picture of the house in Spokane as it appeared during the time the Alstons lived there. The most intriguing item was Mattie's mother's napkin ring. Did Elizabeth Shipley eventually spend time with her daughters again?

While arranging my own trip home from Cohoes, I contemplated the Shipley sisters' preparation and readiness for their move west a century earlier. Anticipating how they traveled, and which route they chose, I tried to empathize with their feelings about leaving their past, physically and emotionally, behind them. How would they look toward the future, the unknown—with uncertainty or excitement? Although automobile travel is not nearly the same as train or stage, my aim was to parallel the Shipleys' likely route as near as possible, minus 100 years of progress.

Getting out of Cohoes was easy; transportation by railroad was *the* way of travel at the time. The adventure would begin at the New York Central and Hudson River Railroad stationhouse at the west end of the White Street Bridge.[3] They would embark in Cohoes, then travel through Albany, Syracuse, Rochester, Buffalo, Cleveland, Toledo and on to Chicago. In Chicago, they would choose from several possible routes to Minneapolis-St. Paul and their subsequent connection with the Northern Pacific Railroad. En route, they would cross the Mississippi for the first time, looking on a river so wide that it dwarfed their hometown rivers, the Mohawk and the Hudson. David would meet the train in Bismarck, Dakota Territory.

The railroad cars were loud and dusty. But the Shipley sisters were traveling in June and thus were awarded the sight of the growing season on the plains. It would be a treat and an eye opener to see their world of deep green trees and wide rivers replaced by open prairies and small washes. Industrial towns gave way to small agricultural communities. As they left Minnesota and entered Dakota Territory, the land began to change drastically. They were in the Red River Valley region, in the bed of a prehistoric glacial lake. Fargo would be the last "big" town they would see before Bismarck.

Gradually, they gained elevation and entered the world at

the center of the United States. What was going through Millie's mind as they drew near Bismarck? It was here that she and David would be married. Would she be married in her traveling clothes or was she going to have the opportunity to change into an outfit bought or made especially for this occasion?

Imagine David Alston's excitement as the engine steamed into Bismarck and Millie stepped off the train. They had not seen each other in years.

As Paul and I made our way into Bismarck on our trip, I tried to imagine the city as it was on June 13, 1881. I breathed the air and imagined what the day was like and what Millie was feeling as she stepped off the train and looked for her 5-foot, 8-inch, brown-haired, blue-eyed husband-to-be. Did he look the same as her mind's eye had remembered? Would he still feel the same about her? After all, she had changed some too. How much longer until they would at last be "home"?

Millie and David were married by Methodist minister James M. Bull. A small family celebration probably followed the ceremony before the couple readied themselves for the journey back to Etchetah in Pease Bottom. They had a choice about how to continue the journey. They could again board the Northern Pacific line after being ferried across the Missouri River (construction of the bridge across the Missouri was still under way in 1881) or they could take a steamer.

Whichever way they chose to continue, they entered a stark, unfamiliar and isolated landscape. The western region of Dakota Territory offered spectacular views of weirdly eroded buttes. This land of new sights included prairie dogs, antelope, bison and elk as well.

If they chose train, the end of the tracks was near Glendive, Montana Territory. From there, they would board a stage to reach Etchetah. The stage and mail route, which followed the north bank of the Yellowstone River, was established in 1877.[4]

If they chose the steamer, they might have embarked on the "Helena," which, according to the *Bismarck Tribune*, "left for the Yellowstone, Monday, (June 27) with a good freight and passenger list." If this had been their itinerary, they probably still would have taken the stage route from Glendive or Miles City to Etchetah. Two other steamers, the "Eclipse" and the "General Terry," left Bismarck for destinations on the Yellowstone River that same week. The *Bismarck Tribune* failed to mention whether either vessel carried passengers. Few steamers navigated between Miles City and points west, and those that did usually carried only supplies.

"*Loading N.P. Transfer, Bismarck.*" *A Northern Pacific train is loaded onto ferry for a Missouri River crossing, spring 1880. F. Jay Haynes photo; Montana Historical Society.*

The south bank of the Yellowstone was a maze of railroad construction. Mattie had no idea that two of the hundreds of men working on that construction later would become important in her life. When the railroad finally was completed on the south bank of the river, there was no bridge across the Yellowstone, so visitors would be ferried to David and Millie's home north of the river, on Froze to Death Creek.

At the time of Millie and David's marriage, an end-of-the-tracks town called Kurtzville had begun to grow on the north bank of the Yellowstone River in Pease Bottom. Kurtzville's transient population supported twenty-three saloons, two boarding houses, two stores, a blacksmith shop and a livery stable. One of the ferries across the Yellowstone also was posted at Kurtzville. The Bottom must have seemed like a pretty populated place when the Shipley sisters arrived on July 2, 1881. The bustling from the railroad construction gave it the face of a center of commerce. One thing was certain: Life here promised to be very different than mill life in Cohoes.

If the Alston homestead was like most of the early homes in Pease Bottom, it would be a one-room log cabin with a dirt floor and a mud or sod roof. A fireplace would stand against one wall or in a corner, but there might not be a stove, in which case cooking would be done in dutch ovens over the fire.

Having made the acquaintance of neighbors and settled in, Millie likely worked to make the cabin more of a home. With Mattie's and Lida's help, she might have incorporated what Mrs. Woolfolk had done in her home near the site of Fort Pease, by covering the inside walls with white cloth and painting them with calcimine. Millie probably never contemplated some of the uses that the cloth she used to weave would have. Perhaps she sectioned off a bedroom or two by hanging curtains. Such privacy would have been a luxury.

Much of what they could not grow or manufacture had to be shipped by steamboat to the landing at Guy's ranch. The Alstons would have a garden for personal use. Most families had at least one cow and several chickens for their milk and egg supplies. David also had a team of horses for the ranch. Washing was done over a fire in the yard; their soap usually was homemade from lye and tallow. Wild plums were plentiful in Pease Bottom—and a local treat; plum puddings were very popular. Residents hunted deer and bison for meat, and the fishing was always good.

Life now would take on the routine of everyday chores, including baking bread, ironing, cooking, sewing, cleaning the house and barn, minding the milk cow and chickens, and tending the fire. Visiting with the few neighbors would offer occasional relief from the hard work.

Ranch life was not for everybody. David's brother, Joseph, returned to Cohoes and married. Life in the West was toilsome, but these people were used to hard work and life here offered new freedoms. Their time was their own and their toil was for themselves. The landscape, though somewhat stark compared with the East, was breathtakingly beautiful in its expanse.

As their first summer in Pease Bottom ended and the surrounding hills changed from green to gold, Millie, Mattie and Lida would harvest carrots, potatoes, beets, parsnips and cabbage from their garden and can them for the winter. Perhaps they would join an August plumming party, crossing the Yellowstone and pitching their tents for three or four days. They would spend the first evening enjoying neighbors' company and singing around the campfire. Then, for the next few days, they would transform the fruits into everything from puddings to plum-butter preserves. This was a time when women could share each other's company away from home and routine.

Vegetables were stored in a cellar and packed in sand; the fruits were put up in preserves; and the meat David would bring in from the hunt was kept in an ice house. The large blocks of ice would be cut in winter from the frozen Yellowstone River. Layers of the ice then were alternated with layers of sawdust and would last the entire season.

These things accomplished, the Alstons would have a little time to enjoy leisure activities while they waited for the snow to arrive. Perhaps they took in the local dance at the Guy ranch. If there were more men than women—which usually was the case—some of the men would have to tie handkerchiefs on their arms and dance as "ladies." The dances began early in the evening and were known to last until 10 o'clock the next morning. You can be sure the Shipley sisters danced all night.

As their first winter in Pease Bottom settled in, Millie was looking forward to the birth of her first child, which would arrive in spring, and was glad to have the company of her sisters. Back in Lowell, Betty Shipley was applying for a widow's pension, a development that had been in the works since about the time Lida joined her sisters in Cohoes. Millie made an affidavit for her mother on August 19, 1881. Betty's daughters were planning to have their mother join them; that their mother's napkin ring was among the possessions left at the house in Spokane convinced me of this. There also might have been preparations for a bigger cabin to accommodate the Alston's growing family—if everything would go as planned.

But on a cold Wednesday in January, things took a bit of a turn. On the 18th, David's team of horses ran away and threw him underneath his heavily loaded wagon; his ankle and leg broke as the wagon wheel passed over him. David was unable to work for some time after that, so Millie's, Mattie's and Lida's roles encompassed the heavier, more difficult chores of ranch life: splitting wood, hauling water and supplies, hunting, and clearing snow so the stock could feed—in addition to their usual load of monotonous chores.

Mattie and Lida must have been a big help to the family when, on May 13, 1882, Millie gave birth to her first child, Grace.

Perhaps Mattie even followed in her aunt Martha's footsteps and assisted or was midwife to Millie.

With all the new sights, sounds and responsibilities that came with her first year in Montana, Mattie surely spent time in the town of Kurtzville for recreation. And it was during this first year in Pease Bottom that Mattie met her husband-to-be, Eugene A. Gillett. Mattie obviously was impressed by this 5-foot, 11-inch, brown-haired, brown-eyed, self-assured railroad worker. Eugene was a contractor on construction of the Northern Pacific Railroad. They began courting and, although it was more primitive here than "back East," Mattie and Eugene could find plenty to do. Horseback riding was becoming popular among the ladies, so a ride on the homestead or to survey the railroad construction might have been in order. A visit to Etchetah or Kurtzville for mail and supplies would turn into a pleasant trip for Mattie if Eugene accompanied her. Fishing trips, picnics and dances certainly were on the agenda as well. But summer chores soon would keep Mattie busy again. And she probably would see less of Eugene as construction of the Northern Pacific made its way toward Billings.

Betty Shipley's widow's pension was approved on June 8, 1882. In addition to a pension of $8 per month, she would get retroactive money for the support of Mattie and Lida until they had reached the age of 16. This provided more than enough for the fare to Montana.

On August 17, 1882, construction of the Northern Pacific tracks to Billings was completed. The first passenger train steamed into town at 5:30 p.m., and the same day also found Calamity Jane in town. The city was growing fast and already supported a population of 1,200.

As Mattie's second summer in Montana drew to a close, she was making wedding plans. On October 24, 1882, Mattie and Eugene were married at Millie and David's home in Pease Bottom. Was Millie's dress used with alterations? Or perhaps a dressmaker in Billings helped create the wedding attire. Maybe Mattie made an outfit herself for the special occasion. After all, working with textiles was in her blood.

With Eugene making his residence at the Park Hotel in Billings, Mattie now would leave her family behind. And she would trade some of the hardships of frontier life for the new responsibilities of wife and homemaker.

—————————————————————

[1] Advertisement and map of the Northern Pacific Railroad.

[2] *Tales of Treasure County*, (Treasure County Bicentennial Commission: 1976), p. 33.

[3] Arthur H. Masten, *The History of Cohoes*, (Albany: Joel Munsell, 1877), p. 219.

[4] *Illustrated History of the Yellowstone Valley*, (Spokane, Washington: Western Historical Publishing Company), p. 268.

Chapter 6

Meeting Eugene

$\mathcal{M}$attie's first husband, Eugene Gillett, was the fourth of five children born to David and Mariah Gillett, farmers originally from New York state. Like Mattie's family, however, the Gilletts were not content in their hometown and sought the "better life" elsewhere. Their quest steered David and Mariah to Canada, where their children were born and where the family lived for almost twenty years—from about 1834 to 1853.

But sometime before 1853, David and Mariah split up, and David married or began living with his "new wife," Catherine, who had children of her own. He took all of his and Mariah's children, except their eldest son, Jerome, with his new family, and immigrated to northeast Iowa with other members of his family from New York. They settled on 320 acres in Allamakee County, Iowa. But David was in poor health, which strained the family's finances. He died on January 8, 1857, and the doctor bill during his last illness was $28.50. He probably did not live to see the birth of his last child—his only child with Catherine—Sarah Ellen.

Jerome Gillett settled in central Minnesota, northwest of Allamakee County, Iowa, and was the only one of his siblings to maintain contact with his mother. After David Gillett died, Mariah ventured to Iowa to "reclaim" her children. And by 1860, she had regained custody of Mary Cordelia, Marshall, Eugene

and Marian Gillett. David's youngest child, Sarah Ellen, remained with her mother, Catherine.

David left no will when he died, setting off a wrangle between Mariah and Catherine. Mariah asserted that Catherine sold
much of David's personal property, then left the premises, with the
children under Mariah's care. As a result, Mariah claimed, "the
children had no beds or bedding or other things to provide for their
comfort." She took the issue to court with hopes of winning some
control over her children's inheritance, so as to provide for them.
But the court dismissed the case, reminding Mariah that Catherine
(even though she was not David's lawful widow) was appointed
administratrix and would be liable for any misappropriation of
the estate.

As the Civil War broke out, the Gillett family barely scraped
a living from land that held potential to fulfill all their needs.
Eugene, nineteen, was determined to fight for the Union rather
than abide the ongoing family battles. On August 15, 1862, days
before Mattie's father, George Shipley, enlisted in New York,
Eugene joined the ranks of Company I of the 27th Iowa Infantry as a 4th Corporal. Eugene was mustered in at Camp Franklin,
near Dubuque, Iowa, on September 5, 1862. The mustering officer rejected Eugene's older brother, Marshall W., that same day.

Eugene's company traveled through Minnesota and Illinois
to Tennessee, Mississippi and Arkansas; his regiment engaged
in various duties, among them guarding the lines of the Mem-
phis and Charleston Railroad and the Mississippi Central Railroad. In so doing, Eugene was promoted to 3rd Corporal and
began to demonstrate a knack for the profession with which he
would be associated the rest of his life—railroading.

On March 10, 1864, Eugene was promoted to 2nd Corporal.
This also was the first day that his company engaged in active
battle with the rebels, as they fought to capture Fort DeRussy in
Louisiana:

> "The Twenty-seventh Iowa had in this, its first, battle
> established a record for bravery and efficiency commen-
> surate with that of the other splendid regiments of its
> brigade. Its subsequent history will show how well it
> maintained the honor it had won."[1]

After the battle, Eugene was transferred to the Invalid Corps., having contracted pneumonia and pleurisy in his right lung. These illnesses eventually developed into consumption, with which he would suffer for the rest of his life. Plagued with chronic diarrhea, often a symptom of consumption, Eugene served seventeen more months before being mustered out, as a sergeant, on August 3, 1865, at Davenport, Iowa. Eugene's enlistment had exposed him to a tremendous amount of travel: "During its term of service the Twenty-seventh Iowa marched over 3,000 miles and traveled by steamboat and railroad over 10,000 miles."[2]

During Eugene's military service, his family underwent dramatic change. His mother, who had remarried a year before Eugene enlisted, was ill and died before he was released from duty. Except for his brother Marshall, all of Eugene's siblings had left Iowa, and his stepmother and stepsister had moved to Illinois. The land over which his mother and stepmother fought so bitterly had been sold, except for his interest. With nothing else to keep him in Allamakee County, Eugene sold his remaining rights to the land and moved on to carve out his own future.

After spending some time in St. Croix, Wisconsin, Eugene moved on to Minnesota, where his brother, Jerome, and his father's relatives lived. By then, Eugene might have known that he had serious health problems; traveling was encouraged and accepted as a potential cure for men with consumption. Being an invalid no longer was an attractive occupation for the consumptive. "Health seeking" was the new cure and, if it included an outdoor work regime that enabled a man to "Come West and Live," all the better.[3] Health seekers accounted for a good portion of Western immigrators.

Eugene already possessed the skills necessary for a traveling work cure. It didn't take him long to find work with the railroad, and thus began the chapter of his life that would land him in Montana. In 1866, the Southern Minnesota Railroad Company was making rapid progress laying rails across Fillmore County, Minnesota, and Eugene jumped at the chance to work for the company. He had been living in Winona, Minnesota but now would be on the move as the railroad progressed across the southern part of the state.

In 1867, rails were being laid from Houston, in Houston

County, to Rushford, the first town across the line into Fillmore County. Railroad construction in this area would remain at fever pitch for the next few years. By 1868, the rails had progressed across a third of the county, from Rushford to Lanesboro; the next year, a branch line was completed from Ramsey to Wells. By 1870, the main line stretched from Lanesboro to Ramsey, and a branch from Fountain to Chatfield was under construction. During this evolvement, Eugene lived at the railroad boarding house of Russell Hart in Carrollton, Minnesota.

Eugene advanced to railroad overseer for the Southern Minnesota Railroad Company, with at least thirteen workers under his supervision. Most of his laborers were from Canada, Ireland and Sweden, with only one man from the United States. While working in Fillmore County, Eugene was relatively close to several members of his family: His older brother, Marshall, was south of him in Allamakee County, Iowa; Jerome was northwest of him in Stearns County, Minnesota; and several of his father's relatives were north of him in Wabasha County, Minnesota. But as rail work advanced through the state, Eugene would leave his

Big Cut and Sweet Briar Valley, Dakota Territory, 1879. It's easy to imagine Eugene Gillett and Ellery working on a cut like this for Northern Pacific Railroad.

family behind. Completely on his own now, he would seek better health and work—and a bride.

When the Northern Pacific Railroad reorganized, Eugene began working for that company, advancing to the position of contractor. By 1880, he was working on the section of track making its way through western Dakota Territory. That year, he was listed—along with hundreds of other laborers—in the census of what then was Billings County. Among those laborers was a man named Ellery Culver. Because hundreds of people were working on the construction, Eugene and Ellery might not have known each other. Imaginative and capable, though, Ellery Culver was a striking figure of a man, and Eugene was highly visible in his position. I like to imagine them crossing paths.

As construction of the Northern Pacific Railroad progressed from Dakota to Montana Territory and into the Pease Bottom area, train officials eyed the town of Coulson, Montana for a potential railroad hub. An early settler of the town, Perry W. "Bud" McAdow, realized the importance that a railroad would have for the region and encouraged the idea. Another prominent man, John J. Alderson, filed a town plat for Coulson and launched its first real-estate operation. Other businesses then began springing up, many under 12-foot-by-16-foot canvas tents. Two doctors, two dentists and two lawyers set up shop, amid the typical dry-good and hardware stores, restaurants, and the ever-present saloons and dance halls that lined the streets.

Meanwhile, the Minnesota and Montana Land and Improvement Company—the construction arm of Northern Pacific—tried to persuade McAdow and Alderson to pare the price of their property. Unable to sway the two men, however, the company acquired land north of Coulson and founded its own town, naming it for Northern Pacific's Frederick Billings.

In April of 1882, Heman Clark, of the Minnesota and Montana Land and Improvement Company, announced the establishment of Billings, Montana. Numerous businesses transferred to the new city immediately, knowing that prosperity would be where the railroad was. Nonetheless, others remained in Coulson, loyal to their hometown, which proceeded to lose its post office on June 13, 1882. Surely, McAdow and Alderson were unnerved.

During this time, Eugene Gillett was subcontracting for Northern Pacific with a partner, under the name "Gillett and Fritz." He then teamed with another partner, Joseph Laundrie, under the name "Gillett and Laundrie." In March, Eugene Gillett and Joseph Laundrie began grading and building portions of the railroad bed for the Northern Pacific section that would pass through Billings and Coulson. They worked for Heman Clark, then doing business as "H. Clark and Company." But on July 23, 1882, Eugene Gillett and Joseph Laundrie dissolved their partnership, by mutual accord. Their agreement included payment of a note, held by H. Clark and Company, to Eugene Gillett, in exchange for his half interest in the partnership.

Meantime, work to raise Billings got under way. Creating a ditch to supply the town with water was among the essential undertakings. The canal was designed to divert 20,000 inches of water from the Yellowstone River, a project so extensive that it became known as the *Big Ditch*. I.D. O'Donnell, of Billings, was in charge of construction, and Eugene subcontracted independently for work on the ditch. And although he was working hard, his coming marriage to Mattie Shipley—just three months away—likely was foremost in his mind. Like many other railroad workers, Eugene was living at the Park Hotel in Billings, but he would have to provide a home for his new wife soon.

In organizing his future, one of Eugene's first tasks was to collect his money from H. Clark and Company. The explanation of his dissolution agreement with Joseph Laundrie was simple:

H. Clark & Co.
Contractors,
Extension Northern Pacific R.R.
Montana Territory
Billings M.T. July 23, 1882

E.A. Gillett
    We will pay you on Mr. Joseph Laundrie's order thirty days from date the sum of $2387.50. We understand that you sell him one half interest in 11 teams and this document is given to us as your payment on presenting his order at the time specified.

Respectfully yours
H. Clark and Co.[4]

Unfortunately, Heman Clark was not at the office the day Eugene called to collect his money. Eugene called back several times but did not see Heman Clark until August 28. Clark then gave Eugene $500 of the amount due, and Eugene signed for it on the back of the document. Little did Eugene know that his troubles were just about to begin. Joseph Laundrie had signed another document placing a condition on the payment to Gillett, but Eugene had not been present when that document was executed. It read as follows:

> H. Clark & Co.
> Contractors
> Extension Northern Pacific R.R.
> Montana Territory
> Billings M.T. July 23, 1882
>
> Messrs. H. Clark and Co.: Please pay to Mr. E.A. Gillett thirty days from date the sum of Two thousand two hundred eighty seven dollars fifty cents (2287.50) under the condition that any difference of the late copartnership be deducted thereof.
>
> Joseph Laundrie[5]

Eugene would have to fight for the balance of his money in court. But he did not pursue the issue until nearly a year later because he was immersed in his new life with Mattie.

---

[1] Wm. H. Thrift, "Historical Sketch of the Twenty-Seventh Regiment, Iowa Volunteer Infantry," *Roster and Record of Iowa Soldiers in the War of the Rebellion,* (Des Moines, Iowa: E.H. English, 1908-1911), p. 1122.

[2] Ibid. pp. 1125-1126.

[3] Sheila M. Rothman, *Living in the Shadow of Death, Tuberculosis and the Social Experience of Illness in American History*, (New York, New York: Basic Books, 1994), p. 148.

[4] Court records, Custer County, Montana, Gillett vs. H. Clark & Co., Exhibit "A".

[5] Court records, Custer County, Montana, Gillett vs. H. Clark & Co., Exhibit "B".

Chapter 7

Love and Law

It is curious that Mattie claimed in her wedding announcement to be from Philadelphia, considering that she lived there such a short time. Perhaps it would elevate her social status in Billings to shed the "working class" image associated with Cohoes.

"Married
GILLETT—SHIPLEY. Oct. 24, at residence of Mr.
David Alston, in Pease Bottom, E.A. Gillett, of Billings
to Miss Mattie J. Shipley, of Philadelphia."[1]

Eugene A Gillett   Mattie Gillett

Like all first-time brides, Mattie certainly looked forward to her wedding day, with hopes that it would be perfect. Tuesday, October 24 would begin clear, cool and sunny. David and Millie's home would be decorated for the occasion. Mattie's family would surround her and, after a flawless ceremony, send her on her way with their blessings. She and Eugene would board the train to Billings, their gifts and good wishes in tow. Although Mattie may have been sorry to leave her siblings, the excitement of her own first love and home would drown the pain of separation.

Mattie made new friends in Billings, including Abbie S. Lee,

a teacher. It was Abbie who wrote the only entry from Montana
in Mattie's autograph book, on April 17, 1883:

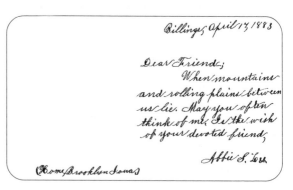

*Mattie made a
"devoted" friend
quickly in Mon-
tana and hon-
ored her by ask-
ing Abbie to sign
the autograph
book.*

But Abbie's autograph was the last entry in Mattie's book.
Did a more complicated life take away Mattie's time and inno-
cence? Did she put away such girlish pleasures as autograph shar-
ing? Or did she stop using the book because parting sentiments
were becoming the theme?

The Billings Herald announced Abbie's departure four months
after she signed Mattie's book:

> "Miss Abbie Lee, who has so efficiently taught our
> public school for some months past, has been obliged to
> cease teaching on account of her health. She will start in
> a few days with some friends on a trip through the park;
> after which she proposes to return to the east. We trust
> she will reconsider the last intention as she is highly es-
> teemed in this town for her social qualities as well as her
> abilities as a teacher."

Had Abbie Lee also been a "health seeker" in Montana? Did
she pursue the "man's cure" when she took a teaching job so far
away from her Iowa home? Her trip through the park took a
month; maybe it also was part of her cure before returning East.

Mattie and Eugene also made their own trip into Yellowstone
Park. The National Park Tourists Record of Mammoth Hot
Springs shows them registered on July 10, 1883. With them was
J.S. Munson, also of Etchetah. Evidently Mattie and Eugene were

hoping the park's atmosphere would relieve his lung problems since he was listed as an invalid in the record book.

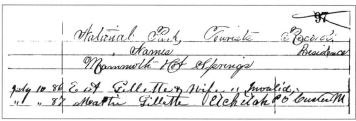

The Mammoth Hot Springs register, July 10, 1883.

August, 1883 marked a turning point in Mattie's life. Not only did she say goodbye to a friend, but Eugene's health became critical. The lung ailments from which he suffered during the war, coupled with new stress from his encounters with Northern Pacific, were taking their toll. Eugene was diagnosed with consumption.

It had been more than a year since Berlin doctor, Robert Koch, had identified tubercle bacillus as the cause of consumption and changed the name of the disease to tuberculosis. But that discovery would not help Eugene, diagnosed in the third and terminal stage of the disease. An early noted American doctor, William Sweetser, described some of the symptoms of this final stage:

> "The cheeks are hollow.... The eyes are commonly sunken in their sockets ... and often look morbidly bright and staring.... All the comeliness and pleasing symmetry of the human form are destroyed ... wasted away ... graveyard cough or death rattle is distinctive and unmistakable ... pain in the joints ... weaker and accelerated pulse ... uncontrollable diarrhea.... In the majority of instances, the mind maintains its integrity to the last."[2]

This probably was an all-too-familiar scene for Mattie. As consumption was the leading occupational hazard in the textile industry, she knew the outcome. She turned to her family for help, taking Eugene to Pease Bottom for recuperation.

By mid-August, Eugene knew his condition was serious enough to take action for his wife's future. He hired Billings attorney E.N. Harwood to file a complaint against H. Clark and

Company to get the money owed him from the 1882 note of Joseph Laundrie. Eugene went to Billings and filed for pension on August 24, stating that the pneumonia and pleurisy contracted while in the Army had developed into the final stages of consumption. On advice of friends, Eugene was examined by Dr. D.M. Parker of Billings so that Mattie could use the official medical record for his pension, in the event of his death.

Mr. Harwood and Eugene acted quickly. On the same day he filed for pension, Eugene gave a deposition, in case he became too ill to appear in court. What Eugene failed to do, however— even with firsthand knowledge of the havoc it could wreak— was to write a will.

In response to Eugene's complaint, Heman Clark filed a claim of his own, stating that Eugene had been advanced $500 of the contract as a personal loan, that the Laundrie order was a conditional one—using the second document signed by Laundrie as proof—and that the conditions never were met. In fact, Clark said, Gillett actually was in debt to him for $300. This last action was brought before Judge McGinness and a jury on October 26. The jury returned a verdict in Eugene's favor. Unfortunately, the attorneys for H. Clark and Company promised to appeal.

Nonetheless, the verdict offered hope for Eugene's own case against H. Clark and Company. But it likely took further toll on his health and, on October 30, 1883, Eugene Gillett died at Millie and David Alston's Pease Bottom home. This notice appeared in the Billings paper on November 3:

> "We regret that telegraphic intelligence has been received here of the death of E.A. Gillett at Guy's Bluff.[3] Mr. Gillett was well known in Billings and along the line of the Northern Pacific railroad. He has been in a dying condition for many months, but his decease will be none the less deplored by a large circle of friends."

Presumably, Eugene was buried in the lower Pease Bottom cemetery. Over time, however, the Yellowstone River, in changing course, eroded the bank where the cemetery rested. Most of the graves were moved, but others washed away, leaving no trace. No record or stone remains to mark Eugene's life and passing.

Married only one year and six days, Mattie suddenly found herself alone. Eugene had owned some town lots in Billings that would become Mattie's—and then there was his lawsuit. Most important, she had her memories of their short time together.

An incident that might have helped with the lawsuit arose in December. Whatever Joseph Laundrie's reputation in the community, publicity like this was not likely to look good for H. Clark and Company:

"Joe Laundrie, of Terry (Custer County) has been bound over to appear before the grand jury on a charge of horse stealing."[4]

Eugene probably had severed ties with Joseph Laundrie for good reason.

How Mattie made it through the holiday season, we can only guess. One year earlier had been her happiest time. But on December 27, 1883, Mattie was appointed administratrix of Eugene's estate. Instead of a restful period of grief and mourning, Mattie apparently kept quite busy. She was determined not to let Eugene's reputation be tarnished posthumously.

The sight of a comet on January 2, 1884 offered a thrilling beginning to the new year for Mattie. With a pair of field glasses, she would have gotten a good view of the comet in the northwestern sky, just within the Milky Way. A crisp, clear evening opened the wonderments of the universe between the horizon and the zenith.

On March 22, 1884, notice was given that Mattie, as administratrix of Eugene's estate, would apply to the Judge of the District Court to continue the action against H. Clark and Company.

The court case probably gave Mattie a good outlet for her grief. She also was certain to have the support of her family. Perhaps she was even distracted while in Pease Bottom. Planting season was upon the Alstons, and there was always work to be done. Mattie's niece, Grace, was almost 3 years old and sister Millie was pregnant with her next child. The new arrival, Edward Shipley Alston, was born April 25, 1884.

The two Gillett court cases continued. On May 20, H. Clark and Company asked for a continuance of their case. When the motion was overruled, they asked that the case be dismissed without cost to them. That judgment was denied, and the company was required to pay court costs. If the attorneys for H. Clark and Company assumed that Mattie also would consider dismissing her case, they were mistaken. Mattie would not back down.

The summer brought trouble to Billings. On July 14, fire destroyed many businesses, including most of Block 110, as reported by *The Billings Herald*:

"At midnight on Monday the citizens were aroused by an alarm of fire and upon turning out learned with consternation that McKee Bros' building, in the heart of block 110, was on fire. The wind at the time was blowing very lightly, but those who saw the fire at its source expressed the opinion that it was impossible to save McKee's building, if indeed, any building in the block. The attention of every one was therefore, for the time, turned to the salvage of the stocks in the different places of business. So well was this work performed that the greater portion of the goods were removed from all the buildings, but unfortunately as the fire progressed the heat became so intense that those goods which had not been far enough removed became a prey to the devouring element.

"Efforts were made to tear down the buildings on either side of McKee's building with hooks and ropes, but these efforts proving unavailing it was decided to blow up Hefferlin's building which was done. This only seemed to add to the fierceness of the flames which were already spreading to the building owned by Kennard and Fenske on the west and to the building owned by Racek, Goss and Koltes on the east, but it doubtless was the means of saving the Windsor hotel and adjoining buildings as well as Wheatley Bros' barn.

"The fire burnt itself out quickly and before the wind freshened it was confined to the front of block 110. The citizens vied with each other in their attempts to save property and while there was a lamentable lack of organization, much hard and effective work was done. The only theory advanced as to the origin of the conflagration is that a smoldering fire was started by some of the hot metal used by workmen who were engaged during Monday in fixing the tin roof of McKee's building. This opinion is sustained by the fact that several parties in the course of the evening noticed a burning odor which seemed to proceed from the building in which the fire commenced."

With so many of Billings' citizens helping during the fire, it's easy to imagine the women of the town, Mattie among them, serving refreshments where needed and perhaps helping smooth over disagreements that night. Some buildings that were saved included the Post Printing Office, Wheatley Brothers barn, W.F. Eilers building and the courthouse.

As the town struggled to recover from the devastation, Mattie carried on her court case with persistance.

On December 8, 1884, H. Clark and Company asked the court for a change of venue because of alleged prejudice in Billings. Heman Clark's attorney offered information about the company's business transactions in the Minnesota and Montana Land and Improvement Company, the Northern Pacific Railroad and the general store it owned in Billings. He went on to say that Clark, both personally and in business, had other actions pending in the courts of Yellowstone County and:

> "... has always had good cause of action and defenses, in said actions the juries that tried those actions had almost invariably rendered a verdict against the interest of said Clark.... He has resided in the town of Billings in said County almost all the time which said town was organized, during the greater part of which time he has had opportunities of ascertaining the feelings, bias and prejudices of the citizens of said County...."[5]

Clark must have made some enemies in Billings to feel the citizens wouldn't give him a fair trial. Such people would have included men like Perry W. "Bud" McAdow—now a prominent Billings businessman—and John J. Alderson. Heman Clark did not follow through on his promises and did not fulfill his agreements with many businesses. Now he could not count on them.

On December 13, the court changed the venue of the case to
Custer County, and the battle continued. Whether H. Clark and
Company could get an equitable trial in Custer County was a
matter of opinion. Custer County was Mattie's homeground, but
it was Joseph Laundrie's territory too. He lived in Terry and
held a solid social standing there.

Finally, on March 7, 1885, Judge John Coburn of the District
Court in Custer County addressed the jury:

> "First, the Jury are instructed that all material, allega-
> tions of the plaintiff's complaint, which are not specifically
> denied by the defendant's answer stand admitted as true,
> and need no further proof.
>
> "Second, the Jury are the exclusive judges of the cred-
> ibility of testimony, the manner in which the witness tes-
> tifies, the character of the testimony, evidence affecting
> the character of the witness, for truth, honesty and integ-
> rity, the motive of the witness and contradictory evidence
> may also be considered by the Jury in weighing the testi-
> mony of a witness.
>
> "Third, if the Jury believe from the evidence that
> Heman Clark, one of the defendants in this action, and a
> member of the firm of H. Clark and Co. wrote the letter
> set out in plaintiffs complaint and signed the name of the
> firm of H. Clark and Company thereto, and delivered
> the same to plaintiff, and that the plaintiff took the order
> of Joseph Laundrie and parted with his property on the
> faith of such letter, the Jury are instructed that under such
> circumstances the letter promising to pay such order, was
> equivalent to accepting the order in writing.
>
> "Fourth, the Jury are instructed that the acceptor of an
> order of bill of exchange is primarily liable for its payment.
>
> "Fifth, if the Jury believe from the evidence that
> Heman Clark acting as a member of the firm of H. Clark
> and Company wrote the letter set out in plaintiff's com-
> plaint and delivered the same to the plaintiff without
> fraudulent inducement from plaintiff but for the purpose
> of securing the payment of the sum to Gillett, named in
> said letter, on the order of said Laundrie drawn and pre-

sented in conformity with the terms of said letter, and if, the Jury further believes that said Gillett took said order, and parted with his property, on the faith of said letter, and presented said order at its maturity for payment according to the terms of said letter and order, then the Jury will find for the plaintiff.

"Sixth, but if you believe from the evidence that the plaintiff accepted the order to secure the payment for his interest in the property of Gillett and Laundrie with a condition that it was to be paid out of any balance that might be due to that firm from H. Clark and Company and that nothing is due to the firm of Gillett and Laundrie from H. Clark and Company then you should find for the defendant.

"Seventh, if the Jury find for the plaintiff against H. Clark and Company they will find what amount is due upon the order of bill of exchange set out in plaintiffs complaint.

"Eighth, the Jury are instructed that in the event a person or persons have money or other valuable things capable of manual delivery in his or their hands or under their control, which being the subject of litigation, such person claiming no interest in, he may deposit such money or other valuable thing in court, and thereby absolve himself, or themselves from costs in such action."[6]

The jury of twelve men later returned the verdict, presented by foreman W.E. Savage:

"We the Jury find for the plaintiff and assess her damages in the sum of seventeen hundred and eighty seven dollars and fifty cents against H. Clark and Company."[7]

On March 9, the judge ordered H. Clark and Company to pay the amount in the original complaint, plus court costs. H. Clark and Company immediately appealed to the Supreme Court of Montana.

It was nearly another year before the Supreme Court released its decision, which was printed in the Billings paper on January 10, 1886:

"The Supreme Court on the 7th inst. rendered its decision in the case of Mattie Gillett, administratrix against H. Clark and Co., affirming the judgement of the plaintiff. This case has been bitterly contested in the courts of Yellowstone and Custer counties and in the Supreme Court for more than three years, finally resulting in favor of the plaintiff. The suit was commenced by the late Mr. Gillett, and after his decease was revived in the name of his widow and executrix, the present plaintiff. The defendants were the well known contractors. The late Mr. Gillett had, in partnership with the late Joe Laundrie, subcontracted under Clark and Co., but Laundrie interposed a claim and the matter has gone on in litigation until both the original litigants have passed from the jurisdiction of earthly courts. The public will be pleased to learn the widow has gained the suit she so pluckily fought."

This could not have been an easy time for Mattie, even with the support of her family and the courts. But in unwavering pursuit of her rights, Mattie caught the public eye and the praise of the local newspaper. It was during this time that she likely caught the eye of Ellery Culver as well. He was the manager of her Billings residence, the Park Hotel, when the case finally came to a close.

---

[1] *The Billings Herald*, 26 October 1882.

[2] William Sweetser, *Treatise on Consumption.* (Boston: T.H. Carter, 1836), pp. 81-82.

[3] The place names in the Pease Bottom area have changed quite a bit over the years. The area referred to as Guy's Bluff, named after Etchetah's postmaster and first permanent settler, John C. Guy, is now called Hysham Hills according to local residents.

[4] *The Daily Enterprise*, Livingston, Montana; 17 December 1883.

[5] Court records, Custer County, Montana, Gillett vs. H. Clark & Co., Affidavit for Change of Venue.

[6] Ibid., Instructions to the Jury; usually these records are disposed of after a short period of time and only the calendars are kept. I have included the instructions to the jury and the verdict as they were recorded because Custer County, Montana chose to keep these records intact. It is not often a researcher has the opportunity to see the actual words of the past as they were spoken.

[7] Ibid., Verdict.

Chapter 8

Life with Ellery

Ellery Culver's great niece, Freda Beach, provided an essential thread in weaving the yarns of Ellery's life and Mattie's death. And as the tales unraveled, it was fascinating to note the similarities between the two men Mattie married.

Ellery's paternal family—from Connecticut, then Massachusetts, then Vermont—were farmers for generations. When Ellery's father, Eliakim Culver Jr., was born on August 17, 1788, Eliakim Sr. was town clerk and carefully recorded the event himself. Likewise, all of Ellery's aunts' and uncles' births were recorded in the town records of Shoreham, Addison County, Vermont.

Ellery's mother, Eliza Vincent, was born in Shoreham, though her family might have come from England or Ireland. According to Freda Beach, Eliakim Jr. left home as a young man and, with his wife, Eliza, began raising their family in Stockholm, New York, where two of Eliakim's brothers also lived. As Eliakim Sr. grew older and no longer could care for the Shoreham farm by himself, Eliakim Jr. and his family returned to help.

Eliza and Eliakim Jr. were blessed with a large family. Ellery was the eleventh of twelve children. He was born on April 28, 1842, and was named after William Ellery Channing, an influential congregational minister of the day. William Ellery Channing died the same year that Ellery Channing Culver was

born, but Channing's spirituality seemed to guide Ellery throughout his life. Ellery tried to follow the beliefs set by the minister,
who spoke out against slavery and other social abuses and
preached that humans' basic nature was the same as God's. Ellery
was guided by the ethical ideal of perfecting himself while also
helping to foster the progress of society.

Ellery spent his early childhood in Shoreham, east of Lake
Champlain and near the border of Vermont and New York. Its
rolling forested hills offered Ellery and his siblings room to explore. When Ellery was two years old, his mother died while
giving birth to his stillborn sister, Eliza. They were buried in
the family plot in Lake View Cemetery, and Ellery remained
the youngest in the family.

After his wife's death, Eliakim Jr. decided to make a fresh
start for himself and his children. His father had died in 1841,
and Eliakim no longer
felt an obligation to the
family land. He spent
the next few years es-
tablishing his family in
Bellevue, Huron
County, Ohio. But on
October 19, 1849, just
short of Ellery's sixth
birthday, his father
died, leaving the older
siblings to care for the
younger ones.

Ellery Culver (fourth from right) in front of the Cottage Hotel, Mammoth Hot Springs, circa 1895. Yellowstone National Park photo archives.

The parallels between Mattie's and Ellery's childhoods are
obvious. Both initially were brought up by fathers but lost their
fathers at about the same age; both then were under the care of
older siblings until they could make their own way. Shoreham, Vermont also is close to Cohoes, New York, so Mattie's and Ellery's
early memories encompassed the same general environment.

In 1860, eighteen-year-old Ellery was back in Vermont—in
Sudbury, Rutland County, with his sister, Laura Culver Bucklin,
and her husband, Hollis. Ellery remained close to Laura throughout his life. And Laura's grandchild, Freda Beach, would retain
early childhood memories of "Uncle Ellery."

Ellery seemed restless. He returned to Bellevue, Ohio, and joined the Army on July 30, 1861. It was early in the war when he enlisted as a private in Company D, 34th Ohio Volunteer Infantry. He marched into three years of service from Camp Lucas in Ohio. Fortunately, some of the letters that Ellery wrote to his eldest sibling, Thede Rebecca, survived. These letters help us understand who Ellery Culver was; they are awash with portrayals of the attitudes of the day and rich with sentiments of men in war and politics.

In the following letter, dated June 22, 1862, from Flattop Mountain, Ellery talks about the way he and his company dealt with death. He also reveals his longings for home:

"Dear Sister,

Another Sunday morning has come, with its many joys + sorrows. Our Compy is on guard but I was not needed, so I will improve a few moments by writing to you. One of our Company Boys, Joseph Starbuck, Died yesterday about 2 o'clock P.M. + was buried at sunset. Eight of us with Arms, Commanded by Corpl Wright, formed the Escort while the whole Regt followed without Arms. Mr. Gordon who corresponds with the Cincinnati Times + signs his name Volunteer performed the Exercises as the Chaplain is absent. There is but little of interest to write. Every thing goes along finely. Nate Strong + myself were out about a mile the other Day Strawburying we got about a pint. I suppose such stuff is plenty in Ohio. how I would like a meal of Lettuce green Peas +c. Such things are not to be seen in this part of Virginia. Near Barboursville there are some <u>civilized</u> farmers, but up here there is neither farmer or garden. I have not seen one half Dozen women since we left Gauley Bridge.

"Rebecca I Remember of your writing me when at Mudbridge about Swearing. it has got to be one of the worst things in this Regt. Oaths are as plenty as any words in the language Well. The 3rd Article in the Army Regulations says any officer using an oath shall pay one Dollar and for every like offence the same sum to be applied for the sick from the same compy, and every Non commissioned officer or Private who shall use any oath or execration shall pay one sixteenth of a Dollar (16 2/3 cts) and for his second offence he shall not only pay a like sum but be confined 24 hours and for each other offence shall suffer + pay in like manner. Now our Captain has done the best act he Ever did in his life. he has put this Compy down to the fullest extent of that article. <u>I am glad of it,</u> and like him for it. if he stops Swearing in D company it will be the most moral compy in the 34th Regt. for there is no gambling atall in our compy and there is in every other one in the Regt. We have inspection today, but our Compy being on Duty, do not have to go out. Well I must close. Love to all please to answer soon + Remember your Brother E.C. Culver."

On September 10, at Fayetteville, Ellery was shot in the leg. On September 22, he wrote to his sister about his progress:

"I wrote you of my being slightly wounded in the right leg just above the ankle, it is doing first rate + yesterday I even went out doors with the aid of crutches."

Ellery must have been doing "first rate" in his duties as well, because, on December 18, 1862, he was promoted to corporal. Apparently, he found the direction in the military that he was lacking in Vermont or Ohio.

Still, the war was a strain on him and, in an emotional letter to Thede Rebecca, on February 9, 1863, Ellery apologized in closing, saying, "Perhaps I am wrong to thus write my <u>true</u> feelings. If so forgive me. There is not much going on in camp." Ellery questioned his ideas about race, freedom and the politics of war. He began by discussing a book he was reading titled *Harry Burnham*:

"The scenes are in the times of the War of the Revolution. it is Romance founded upon facts. Oh! when I think of our good brave + honored Forefathers that so bravely fought enduring every kind of hardships. Their trials. The treachery of Arnold. + then how bravely they stood everything. it seems as though any person who bears the <u>honorable</u> name of American could willingly Die for their

Country. But then comes the all important question: Are we fighting to free <u>Niggers</u>. Are we shedding the blood of our best friends for a set of accursed Black Men. No. No. I <u>hope</u> not. I like our President's Proclamation. But a set of traitors in the North worse then <u>Benedict Arnold</u> would try to discourage us by saying that it is not constitutional and that <u>they</u> will Rebel if it is not made null + void. The unconditional Union Men leave their Friends, Home + all they hold most dear, + in their abscense the traitors choose their State Officers + then do all they can against us poor Soldiers."

Ellery harbored strong feelings about war and politics throughout his life and remained a member of the G.A.R. post until his death.

Ellery re-enlisted in the military after his initial three-year tour and, on November 24, 1863, began new responsibilities as Brigade Forage Master. He remained on detached duty until July 12, 1864—exactly one year after George Shipley's death—and then returned to his company. Like Eugene Gillett, Ellery climbed the ranks; he was promoted to sergeant on October 17, 1864.

In January, 1865, Major General Sheridan assigned Ellery to the Quarter Master Department at Stephenson Depot, Virginia. After Lee surrendered in April, Ellery waited impatiently for orders to leave; money, women and home were on his mind. On April 21, 1865, he wrote to Thede Rebecca from Stephenson Depot, Virginia:

"Dear Sister,

Your kind letter came to hand this evening + I will immediately reply. I am doing nothing now. Cap't. McCann has been relieved & all of his Clerks are discharged. I wrote you on the 18th inst. concerning this and requested you to forward by Express $80.00 of the money Alonzo Strong drew for me. I do not know when we will receive any pay from the Gov. + I owe some here which it is necessary for me to pay immediately....

"Here comes the Mail Boy with a letter for me from <u>Mollie Huntley</u>. Have read it—no news 'Everything lovely + the goose hanging high.' You please tell Henry he had better look out how he gossips with, 'my Ladie Fair' on the cars. Tell him I hear everything about these affairs + am <u>getting jealous</u>.... Another Rumor is that all the <u>1861 men</u> are going home for three months on half Pay subject to a call at any time. Well! To sum it all up I guess no one knows much about it. I think I shall get home some time this Summer."

Ellery was discharged from service on July 27, 1865, at Wheeling, West Virginia. He returned home but, like David Alston, stayed just a short time before heading for Montana. Here, the similarity between the two men ends, though. Ellery was lured by the gold camps, not by the hope of land, and he went to Virginia City. He might have brought in some money from the gold fields but it's likely that his experience was like that of so many other miners—too many people, high costs for equipment, and long, hard hours. Placer mining might have been simple in theory, but it usually involved more than one miner and, as techniques became more sophisticated, it became more expensive.

Up Alder Gulch was the gold town of Summit. Ellery based there before settling into the bustle of Virginia City. He often stayed at the International Hotel while in Virginia City to pick up mail and attend Masonic Lodge meetings. He was a member of Montana Lodge Number One and was installed as an officer for the quarter ending October 31, 1871.

By 1871, Ellery was established in the city and had fallen into the rhythm of town life. But his wandering streak often took him to remote areas, sometimes for weeks at a time. Later, in Billings, he would take jobs that allowed him time to roam the countryside, as this Virginia City notation from the April 22, 1875 newspaper illustrates:

"E.C. Culver rides to Puller's on horseback in 1 1/2 hours last Saturday."[1]

Puller Springs was a small settlement on the Upper Ruby River, sixteen miles southwest of Virginia City. Ellery must have been proud of the trip or he would not have given the information to the editor for publication. In fact, he enjoyed publicity and would make certain throughout his life that whatever activity he pursued drew notice.

Virginia City possessed the elements necessary to keep merchants busy; miners were always in need of equipment and supplies. And the city offered its inhabitants everything from entertainment to spiritual guidance. Sundays were a celebration of sorts. The stores were open, and thousands of people would crowd the street. Auctions, horse races and prize fights competed with church services. Literary societies, fraternal organizations, opera and theatre abounded, as did saloons, billiards and gambling. Ellery seemed to have everything he could want—but something still was missing for him.

He began to roam farther. The year 1880 found him working alongside Eugene Gillett in Western Dakota Territory, but he also was rumored to have gone as far south as St. Anthony, Idaho to operate a dray system near Henry's Fork. When Mattie moved to Montana, Ellery was living in Glendive, Montana.

Dawson County, Montana was forming at the time and, on September 9, 1881, an official meeting was called in Glendive. Ellery attended and, on his motion, "...A committee of three,

Pen Sketch of Stillwater, Montana. Left to right: Countryman Hotel, Palace Saloon, Culver Saloon, Abbott-Martindale-Allen Store, Norton Store (Line Building). South of track: Alec Countryman home, Wylie home, small shack of Uncle Bill Hamilton.

consisting of Mr. Malony, Mr. Lonergan and E.C. Culver were appointed to draft resolutions to be presented to Governor B.F. Potts."[2]

Among the men running for county office at the time was R.R. Cummings, in the race for superintendent of schools. Ellery and Cummings developed what would become a lifelong friendship, and it was in the presence of R.R. Cummings that Ellery would spend some of the last hours of his life.

Glendive's attractions were not enough to hold Ellery's

attention. Again he began to travel, ending up in Stillwater, Montana, a small settlement on Stillwater or Little Rosebud Creek. Horace Countryman operated a stage station and trading post there as early as 1875, when it was called Eagle's Nest or Sheep Dip. When the Northern Pacific Railroad built a station in 1882 and listed it as Stillwater, Ellery settled there in the saloon business.

The next year marked the beginning of a semblance of permanence for Ellery. In 1883, he married Mamie Jordan; the couple continued to live in Stillwater. Ellery also was in and out of Billings, though, as documented by *The Billings Weekly Herald*:

"March 8, 1883—Messers. Countryman, Pierce, Culver, Nutting and other residents of the western end of the county, were in town on Tuesday."

"Saturday, September 1, 1883—Mr. E.C. Culver, the Isaac Walton of Stillwater, to whom we owe our thanks for several strings of trout, arrived in town last evening."

It's easy to imagine Ellery riding by horseback to Billings and stopping along the way to fish. His gift to the paper ensured him a notice in print.

While Mattie was coping with Eugene's death, Ellery was making plans for a big change in his life as well. Perhaps stemming from his days in Virginia City, he continued his search for precious metals. The "Town Talk" column of the Billings paper reported the following on Saturday, March 29, 1884:

"E.C. Culver of Stillwater spent Tuesday last in town interviewing his numerous acquaintances. Mr. Culver has sold out his business in Stillwater to H. Countryman, and will now take a trip east for the first time in 16 years. Mr. Culver takes with him samples of ores from a number of leads on the head of Stillwater creek in which he is interested and while absent will have them assayed. He is a firm believer in the richness of these leads and predicts a great boom for them in the near future. This opinion is maintained by every experienced miner who has visited the region. Some go as far to say that as soon as it is demonstrated what rich lead this section of country contains, a town will spring up in the neighborhood of Stillwater, that for size and prosperity will lead any place in Eastern Montana."

Ellery must have wanted his relatives in Ohio and Vermont to welcome his new wife to the family. But the couple did not stay long, and their return was announced in the newspaper on Saturday, May 31, 1884:

> "E.C. Culver arrived in town yesterday morning on his way to Stillwater. Mr. Culver has been enjoying a prolonged visit in the east."[3]

Whatever the result of his assay, Ellery never pursued the leads that he was so certain would prove valuable. Instead, the Culvers moved to Billings, and Ellery opened a saloon in June:

> "E.C. Culver, the veteran saloon keeper, has rented W.J. Allason's place in block 110, and opened out with great success on Thursday afternoon. Mr. Culver will keep the very finest brands of goods in his line. With his experience and energy he should meet with good fortune. He has a large circle of friends in this community who will give him their countenance and patronage."[4]

Ellery's timing was unfortunate. When the July 14 fire struck, Ellery's new business went up in flames. He had no insurance, but it did not bankrupt him. He moved into a space in the Farmer's Hotel and continued business as usual. It may have been fate, but the move to the Farmer's Hotel put Ellery in line for a new kind of business. This notice appeared on Saturday, September 6, 1884:

> "E.C. Culver and Charles Wilson have leased the Farmer's Hotel from Mrs. Fitch, and will carry on the business. We trust that they will make a success of it."[5]

Ellery's life continued along the eventful pattern it had followed during the previous few years. Whatever hope Ellery and Mamie had of making a family life in Billings ended on January 9, 1885:

> "We regret to announce the death of Mrs. E.C. Culver which occurred last night, after a short illness. Mrs. Culver who has been a resident of Billings for nearly a year, was surrounded by a wide circle of friends, and her loss will be deeply mourned. Funeral services will take place at the Congregational church tomorrow morning at 10:30."[6]

Mamie was buried in lot 1b in the north half of the Billings Old Cemetery. Perhaps Ellery was feeling too sorrowful to take care of it, but, like Eugene Gillett's, Mamie's grave was never marked with a stone.

Like Mattie, widowed after a short marriage, Ellery immersed himself in city life. He became active in politics, served the court as juror several times, and represented the county commission as judge of election. He was appointed general solicitor for the personal memoirs of U.S. Grant; for this, he traveled from Glendive to Helena canvassing. In addition, he pursued cattle rustlers and served as auctioneer. He also was elected to the "Hook and Ladder Company." Maybe Ellery was following old patterns to help him through his time of grief. Riding the country probably was the best medicine.

At the end of October, 1885, while Mattie was deeply involved in her court action, Ellery became the manager of the Park Hotel, where Mattie lived. If they hadn't crossed paths before, this likely is where they met. Maybe it was fate that drew them together.

Mattie and Ellery were married on April 6, 1886, and so began their short time together. The announcement in the Billings *Daily Gazette* reads:

> "Last evening Mr. Ellery C. Culver was married to Mrs. Mattie A. Gillette, both of Billings. The ceremony was performed by Rev. Alfred Brown, Episcopal rector,

in the presence of a limited number of friends. Congratulations and best wishes are extended by the GAZETTE."

---

[1] *The Montanian*, Virginia City, Montana; 22 April 1875.

[2] *History of Montana* (Chicago: Leeson; Warner, Beers & Company, 1885), p. 541.

[3] "Town Talk," *The Billings Herald*, 31 May 1884.

[4] *The Billings Herald*, 7 June 1884.

[5] "Town Talk," *The Billings Herald*, 6 September 1884.

[6] "Town Talk," *The Billings Herald*, 10 January 1885.

Chapter 9
At Home in Billings

Shortly after Mattie and Ellery married, Millie and David Alston moved their family to Spokane, Washington. Certainly this was difficult for Mattie, amid her already tumultuous life, but Pease Bottom was becoming more arid every year, and crops were more difficult to grow. The spring of 1886 was exceptionally dry, and things were tough for the Alstons. Only the collection of bones from slaughtered bison carcasses was bringing in money, and Millie was pregnant again. Rumor abounded about mining work in the area of Spokane Falls; perhaps David could provide better for the family a little farther west.

This photo of miners was found in the Alston house in Spokane. One of these men likely is David.

When Millie and David left for the more secure life that they hoped the city could offer, Mattie said good-bye to what remained of her past, her life in Cohoes. If Betty Shipley had not already joined the Alston family in Etchetah, she was living in the household by the time they reached Spokane.

Back in Billings, Mattie and Ellery moved into a house of

their own on the south side of town. On May 1, 1886, Ellery started anew in business by buying half interest in Eugene McKee's saloon. The Culvers participated in the Fourth of July celebration, with Ellery serving as marshal of the day. The ladies of St. Luke's Episcopal Church, where the Culvers were married, used McKee and Culver's building for a melon party. They served supper, and a brass band entertained the crowd.

Not all of the Culvers' activities centered around city life, though. Ellery went out on horseback for various reasons, including hunting and fishing. Based on her track record, we can be sure that Mattie was quite capable of holding down ranching life, as well as handling city affairs.

Ellery and Mattie shared outdoor recreation as well, as reported in the Billings paper on October 5, 1886:

> "John Smith, H.H. Bole, E.C. Culver and their wives, started out this morning on a hunting expedition up Pryor River."

This was no small achievement. The usual horseback riding style of women in those days—unless you were Calamity Jane or dared criticisms of the social norm—was sidesaddle. So consider the conditions when one week later, on October 12, the paper reported:

> "H.H. Bole, John Smith, E.C. Culver and their wives (who) have been hunting and fishing up Clarke's Fork and Rocky Creek, returned last evening. Though the last few days were uncomfortably moist, they had a good time and feel much invigorated by their trip."

After the intense heat and drought of the summer, the autumn rain was welcomed. But everyone was predicting a hard winter: Cattle had heavier coats than usual; geese, ducks and other migratory birds headed south much earlier than usual; and, for the first time in many years, the white Arctic owl was seen on the range, which the Indians said would bring a cold winter.

It did. The winter of 1886-1887 was hard on everyone, especially the homesteaders, but the Culvers got by in Billings.

Mattie and Ellery spent the winter preparing for the arrival of their first child. They filled their leisure time with social activity. Ellery was elected an officer of the new G.A.R. McPherson post (the name later was changed to the John A. Logan post, when it was discovered that the Butte G.A.R. post also was named McPherson.) A bit of fun also helped pass the winter months, as evidenced by this report in the Billings paper:

"The handsome album offered by E.H. Lee to the person who guessed nearest to the exact number of seeds in the pumpkin was won by E.C. Culver. His guess was 474, and there were 482 seeds."[1]

Still, the hard winter of 1886-1887 would hold Mattie close to the homefront most of the time. Certainly, letters passed between Spokane Falls and Billings during those harsh months—letters offering love, support, and advice for a sister and daughter going through her first pregnancy at thirty years of age. Ellery had no experience in childbirth either; he and Mattie were learning as they went.

A welcome event brought much excitement for Billings' residents on January 31, 1887: "The Halo That Now Surrounds the Magic City—Another Great Stride in the Progress of Billings—Successful Operation of the Electric Light."[2] To Mattie, it probably seemed like a lifetime since Thomas Edison had invented the incandescent lamp; it was when she lived in Cohoes.

As spring approached, Mattie and Ellery were ready for the addition to their family. Other big transformations were in store as well. On April 25, 1887, Ellery, in line for a new job, dissolved his partnership with Eugene McKee.

Mr. E.C. Waters, an acquaintance of Ellery's, was manager of the Yellowstone Park Association and hired Ellery as its master of transportation. Ellery's old friend from Glendive, R.R. Cummings, who now lived in Miles City, was superintendent of construction for the same organization. Ellery would be in charge of bringing together the construction materials for hotels in Yellowstone National Park; R.R. Cummings would be his superior, and his close friend.

The Billings paper, which was meticulous about such news, never reported visits from Mattie's family at the time of her first child's birth. Ellery might have left for Yellowstone sooner if Mattie had had someone with her but probably was delighted to delay his departure to hold Mattie's hand—and, of course, to pass out cigars in town. Ellery and Mattie named their daughter Theda, after Ellery's oldest sister and his grandmother. Two announcements appeared in *The Billings Gazette*, both on the same day:

"BORN

CULVER—At Billings, Montana Ter., on Wednesday, June 22, to Mr. and Mrs. E.C. Culver, a daughter."

"CITY AND COUNTY

The home of E.C. Culver on the south side of town was made happy this morning by the birth of a little girl."

Mattie obviously came through the delivery well—as did Theda—because on July 2, 1887, just ten days after the birth, Ellery left for his duties in Yellowstone. This Fourth of July would be the most momentous of Mattie's life; she would celebrate with her brand new baby daughter! The entire month of July would be extremely busy for Mattie, as she learned how to be a mother and prepared to follow Ellery to Firehole Basin in Yellowstone National Park.

In 1886, the Yellowstone Park Association took over the Marshall Hotel (sometimes called Marshall's Place or Marshall's House) at the Firehole River and Nez Perce Creek—the "forks of the Firehole."[3] George Marshall had built a mail station and a small summer structure, or "hotel," west of the forks in 1880. In 1884, he ob-

Marshall's Place (Lower Geyser Hotel), near the junction of Nez Perce Creek and Firehole River, 1884. F. Jay Haynes photo; Montana Historical Society.

tained a lease for a site near the mouth of Nez Perce Creek:

"George W. Marshall, the proprietor of the 'Marshalls' in the National Park, has returned from Washington and says he has secured a lease for ten years to the ground he is now occupying at Firehole Basin."[4]

Marshall ran his new hotel in partnership with George G. Henderson, until he sold his interest to Henderson on April 27, 1885. On June 9 of that year, Henderson sold half interest to Henry E. Klamer, and the two ran the hotel jointly until it passed to the Yellowstone Association in 1886.

With the operation transferred to the Association, Ellery was in charge of the construction materials for the log cabins being built on both sides of the hotel. These cabins had eight rooms each, were 16 feet square with 10-foot ceilings, and had the luxury of outside windows.

What Mattie could expect for her family at the forks of the Firehole was described by two tourists of the time. One gentleman adventurer reported:

> "At the forks of the Firehole, two of the roads to the principal attractions of the park converge. There is quite a fair hotel here which is used as a stage station, and also a store at which canned provisions and other supplies needed by camping parties can be obtained. The prices are higher than in Bozeman, seventy-five cents a can for peaches, twenty-five cents for a cigar etc. Still they have to be transported a long distance, and the season for sales is short. The river is a still but swift stream, a hundred feet or so in width. Its source is in the Geysers and in the hot springs along its bank; consequently it is as warm as an ordinary warm bath."[5]

And a woman who entered the park from the west boundary, described it like this:

> "The descent to Firehole Basin, six or seven miles, was made in less than two hours through a thick pine forest. When the brake was applied, at the top of the last slide down hill, we took our first look at Geyserland. We saw at our feet a small story-and-a-half hewn log house, the first hotel built in Yellowstone National Park. A few

rough sheds and a tent adjacent formed the settlement, lying at the base of a steep cliff covered with tall pines. A brook of cold water coursed near the buildings."[6]

One person sees a small log house with a few rough sheds and another sees a fair hotel; we can only guess how Mattie viewed her summer and early autumn accommodations. Sarah Marshall had stayed in that first dwelling with her husband, George, through the winter of 1880-1881 and gave birth to the first white child born in Yellowstone Park. If she could do that, certainly Mattie could stay three months in the "luxury" of a much more refined hotel.

On the morning of July 28, with Theda just one month and six days old, Mattie left on the "No. 1" train to join Ellery in the park. She and Theda traveled west to Livingston, then south to Cinnabar, a 51-mile journey that would take at least three hours. The morning might have been cool to start, but as the day continued through Paradise Valley, the temperature in the shade was 82 degrees. It probably was warmer yet in the train, the dirt and noise unbearable for a 5-week-old baby. As they traveled through Yankee Jim Canyon, then passed Devil's Slide and neared Cinnabar, Mattie probably was relieved to be close to the end of the park branch line of the Northern Pacific Railroad. When they got off the train, they took a stage for eight miles to Mammoth Hot Springs, where they likely stayed the night.

The next day, the journey would take Mattie and Theda some 40 miles farther, to the forks of the Firehole. The road was considered good, and the distance could be covered in one day. Mattie may have chosen to travel by stage, as a tourist, so she could take in the sights as she went.

According to one 1886 description, the trip would have been like this: The first day would be spent at Mammoth Hot Springs, visiting the terraces and pools. If time permitted, another day could be devoted to visiting the falls of the Gardner River, particularly the Middle Falls (Osprey Falls). On the third day, moving toward the Firehole River, you would see Terrace Pass and Swan Lake, cross the Middle Fork of the Gardner River, arrive at the upper end of Willow Park, and continue on to Apollinaris

Spring. The stages would stop here to let passengers quench their thirst with the mineral-laden water. Continuing on, travelers would enjoy Obsidian Cliffs, Beaver Lake, Lake of the Woods, and Hot Springs (Roaring Mountain) before arriving at Norris Geyser Basin to dine and spend two hours examining the geysers and mud pots. Three miles farther on, they would arrive at Geyser Creek and the forks of the Paint (Artists Paint Pots). The head of Gibbon Canyon and the foot bridge to the trail to Monument Geyser Basin are barely one mile farther.

About four miles from the Monument Geyser Basin trail are the Falls of the Gibbon River, which undoubtedly reminded Mattie

Gibbon Falls, 1888. F. Jay Haynes photo; Montana Historical Society.

of Cohoes Falls on the Mohawk River.

Just ten miles farther, Mattie and Theda would arrive at the place that they would call home until late October. In those last miles, the views would include Earthquake Cliffs, Lookout Terrace, National Park Mountain and Firehole Falls.

Spending the late summer months caring for Theda, Mattie had access to the sights of the Upper and Lower geyser basins. Perhaps she did some horseback riding or hiking near the hotel, when she was able to slip away from housekeeping duties. Visiting with the tourists could keep her informed of the "outside world." I like to imagine Mattie enjoying a visit from family members as well; she could show off her first child and meet her newest niece—Millie and David's last child, Mildred, who was less than a year older than Theda.

As autumn approached, the Culvers prepared to return to Billings. On October 24, they were back in the city, and by November 3, they had rented a house on 25th Street for the winter. They quickly re-established city routine. St. Luke's Episcopal, where they were married, was building a new church on the corner of 29th Street and First Avenue South. During construction, services were held in the Park Hotel—a familiar place for Ellery and Mattie to attend, if their habits included church going. Ellery also was involved in organizing a local militia company, and the Culvers attended the G.A.R. masquerade ball. As easily as they had slipped into the park environment, they slipped back into city life.

---

[1] *The Billings Daily Gazette*, Tuesday, 28 December 1886.

[2] *The Billings Daily Gazette*, Monday, 31 January 1887.

[3] According to Lee Hale Whittlesey's *Wonderland Nomenclature: A History of the Place Names of Yellowstone National Park* (Records Management Bureau, Department of Administration; Helena: State of Montana, 1989, text-fiche), pp. 1267-1269, 13F9-13F11. "Chittenden stated in 1895 that the stream was named Nez Perce in 1878 by the USGS, but in a letter to Chittenden, geologist Arnold Hague explained that the name Nez Perce Creek was his own suggestion."

[4] *The Daily Enterprise*, Livingston, Montana; 20 February 1884.

[5] George W. Wingate, *Through the Yellowstone Park on Horseback* (New York: O. Judd Co., 1886), p. 96.

[6] Mrs. Mary B. Richards, *Camping Out in the Yellowstone* (Salem: Newcomb & Gauss, 1910), p. 20.

Chapter 10

— *Yellowstone: Mattie's Final Days* —

That winter in Billings seemed mild compared to the previous year and probably passed quickly for Mattie as she focused her energy on Theda. Meanwhile, Ellery served as juror and in various functions with the G.A.R. post. Mattie and Ellery celebrated their second wedding anniversary in the spring and were looking forward to their second summer in Yellowstone. Before returning to the park, however, Mattie served on the Flower Committee for the G.A.R. Decoration Day memorial services.

Having one summer in the park under her belt, Mattie would have a better idea what she would need to take along this time. And now that Theda was a bit older, Mattie could enjoy the sights more—and Theda's reactions to the fabulous wonders.

"Wonderland" was full of excitement this last year in Mattie's life. The Culvers were among the last ones to witness the eruption of what some called the greatest marvel in Yellowstone— Excelsior Geyser.[1] Ellery wrote the following description of the eruptions that year for *The Billings Gazette:*

> "The Excelsior Geyser is beyond any doubt the largest one in the world. While there are quite a number of others in the National Park, much larger than any outside of its limits, the Excelsior is greatest of them all. Last

spring, and until away along into the summer it played nearly every hour, throwing a body of water 22 feet in diameter, 300 feet high. The crater from which this immense volume of water is forced is in that great wonder 'Hell's Half-Acre.' The latter is a great seething, boiling mass of water, 300 by 500 feet in size, from which a large stream is continually flowing into the West fork of the Firehole river."

Excelsior Geyser, 1888. F.J. Haynes photo, Denver Public Library, Western Collection.

Not to be outshined that summer, of course, was Theda's first birthday. Very few children lived in the park, Theda being perhaps the only one in the Lower Geyser Basin. As such, she no doubt was spoiled a bit by the adults there. Certainly Mattie would appreciate the attention lavished upon her child—especially considering the way she must have been feeling.

For during that summer, it became apparent that Mattie was seriously ill; she recognized the symptoms as those of consumption. She had lived through it again and again—in Cohoes and then, of course, with Eugene. Mattie might have been exposed to tuberculosis during any or all of those times. It's even plausible that symptoms of the sickness prompted her move west with Millie. Certainly, she was in the second stage of the disease that summer, if not the third. Her cough was severe, and she would experience periodic fevers, giving her a ruddy complexion. A continual hoarseness would make it painful to eat or to speak in anything but a whisper. Neither she nor Ellery could fail to recognize her illness.

Treatments for tuberculosis were many but there was not yet a cure. Traveling to a different climate still was considered the "man's cure," while women just continued in the domestic role and hoped for remission. Recognizing that tuberculosis was communicable, people's attitudes about the disease had slowly begun to change; guided by fear, many were convinced that isolation of those infected was the answer. Others believed that the thermal areas in Yellowstone could bring relief for, and possibly cure, the respiratory problems. Perhaps this is what prompted Ellery to accept the winter-keeper position at Firehole Hotel after his summer duties were completed.

Living in the park and caring for her family for two summers taught Mattie the art of compromise and how to make do with the supplies at hand. But the winter would be more difficult. A small bath house that channeled hot water from one of the thermal pools would be the extent of "conveniences." It would be severely cold; the snow would accumulate quickly, and the isolation would be extreme. Mattie would have to plan carefully, as they could haul no supplies in after winter hit. If nothing else, it was comforting to know that soldiers were stationed nearby and that a telephone was available, in case of emergency.

Certainly Theda's needs were foremost in Mattie's mind as she planned for the winter, but she would have to anticipate her own medical requirements as well.

Ellery traveled back and forth between the park and Billings during the summer and early fall, but it is unclear whether Mattie accompanied him on these trips. Ellery's first trip back to Billings was on August 31, when he returned to help the Republican Party prepare for the upcoming presidential election. The Billings paper reported his return:

> "Our old friend E.C. Culver who has been in the Park all season, returned to Billings last Friday, just in time to see the Republican party start off in good shape. He is strong in saying that the Republican party will 'get to the front' in fine shape this fall."[2]

Ellery stayed at least a week to attend the Republican Convention of Yellowstone County. On September 13, he was elected as alternate delegate to the convention. Shortly thereafter, he rejoined Mattie and Theda in Firehole Basin.

Perhaps Ellery made a special effort to be back in Firehole Basin by September 18, Mattie's 32nd birthday, and destined to be her last. As fall approached, Ellery and Mattie shared a month together in the park. They watched the animals grow heavy winter coats and listened to the elk deliver their ritual mating bugles. But in late October, the newspaper again reported Ellery's arrival in Billings:

> "E.C. Culver, in charge of transportation in the Yellow-stone Park, arrived from the west last Sunday. Mr. Culver is here to work in the interest of the Republican ticket."[3]

The election was November 6, and Ellery's candidate, Benjamin Harrison, won the presidential election via the electoral college. After being separated from his family for about two weeks, Ellery returned to the park:

> "E.C. Culver, who has been in Billings during the past fortnight will return to Yellowstone Park today. He intends to winter in the Firehole Basin and during the winter will furnish the Gazette readers with some interesting articles descriptive of Wonderland in midwinter."[4]

Ellery left Billings as the season's first dusting of snow hit the ground. Perhaps he took some special food for the holidays. Did he know this would be his last Thanksgiving, Christmas and New Year's with Mattie?

As the temperatures dropped and the snow piled high, Ellery kept his promise to *The Billings Gazette* by writing about what the park was like in deep winter. In so doing, he also gave us a record of Mattie's last experiences:

> "To the Billings Gazette:
> [Wonderland News]
> Lower Geyser Basin, January 2, 1889. The Yellowstone Park is certainly worthy of deep study at any time, and

especially in 'mid-winter.' The ground at the present writing is covered at this place with twenty inches of snow, and we have less here than at any other hotel in the Park, except Mammoth. They are situated at an altitude 850 feet lower than we are here. It is a strange sight and very beautiful, to see the heavy frost that gathers almost every night on the trees, telephone wire, and in fact everything. It is the frozen steam from the almost countless hot springs in our vicinity. We often see the telephone wire as thick as a man's wrist. Usually this frost all disappears by ten or eleven o'clock. We can see at almost any hour a great cloud hanging over the Excelsior, and other large geysers. It is hard to distinguish these clouds from the other ones floating in the sky. . . .

"There have been four of the Association's teams through the Park this month putting up ice for use at the different hotels. They are under the supervision of R.R. Cummings of Miles City, who for the past two seasons has been master mechanic for the Yellowstone Park Association. They had pretty hard work coming from Mammoth Hot Springs to Norris Geyser Basin. It took them two days, and they were obliged to camp out one night.

"We are 7,150 feet above sea level at this place. Nearly one mile higher than Billings. There is quite a difference in the temperature between the day and night time. On the morning of the 26th ultimo at half past seven it was 32 degrees below zero; at four p.m. it was 8 degrees above. That was the coldest that we have seen so far this winter.

"The eclipse was total at this place. It was for 57 seconds perfectly total, and was a most beautiful sight. Mercury fell seven degrees in 30 minutes at the time."

It's comforting to know that Mattie was amid such a spectacular wonderland during the final months of her life. An eclipse of the sun certainly added more thrill to her memories.

We cannot pinpoint exactly when Mattie's health took a turn for the worse. But because Ellery took no more time to write to *The Billings Gazette*, we can assume that he was too busy caring for Mattie and Theda, in addition to carrying out his job.

Mattie died on March 2, 1889, more than a month shy of her and Ellery's third wedding anniversary. Her tombstone says that she was thirty years old, but Mattie actually was thirty-two when she died. The first public information about her death appeared in *The Billings Gazette* on March 7, 1889:

> "Rumor has it that Mrs. E.C. Culver, formerly known as Mrs. Gillett in the early days of this city, has died at the National Park, of quick consumption, while residing there with her husband who is in the employ of Col. E.C. Waters. It is sincerely hoped that the report is without foundation for by the death of Mrs. Culver society loses a bright star, and her husband and family a true and loving wife and mother."

The following notice, which appeared in the Livingston paper, points up the inaccuracies that often occur in the translation of information:

> "We learn with regret that Mrs. E.C. Culver, well and favorably known to many Livingston and Billings people, died at Mammoth Hot Springs last week. She leaves a husband, Mr. Ed. Culver, master of transportation in the Park, and several children, who lose in her a devoted mother. The bereaved family have the sympathy of the community in their loss of so estimable a wife and mother."[5]

Aside from the inaccuracies, it is interesting that the article states that Mattie was known to Livingston residents as well as those in Billings. Perhaps she traveled with Ellery on business, or maybe Livingston was a stopover for them on their leisurely outings.

By linking several of the available stories about Mattie's death, we can paint a clearer picture of just what happened that March. The work of Aubrey Haines—drawn from oral interviews and written accounts—was the first place I read about Mattie's death:

> "The men at the nearby soldier station gave Culver what help they could. The ground was too deeply frozen

to make a burial at that time, so they brought over two barrels which they set end to end and covered with snow to hold Mrs. Culver's body until a grave could be dug later."[6]

And this account was written by a park visitor in 1901:

"An elderly, comfortable looking official provided by the Park Association, steps into the car and in well chosen words calls the attention of the tourist to the various points of beauty. Listening to his calm, even tones and noting his kindly countenance, one would not suspect that this man had passed through an ordeal so trying that but few men have felt the agony that must have been his.

"Away back in the early days this man had remained one winter in charge of one of the so-called hotels. With him was his young wife and their only child. Along in the winter the wife was stricken with sickness and the anxious husband saw her fade away, until at last inexorable death laid claim to her. With his own hands he dug for her a grave out of the deep snow and ice and to this day, while all know the story of his faded dreams, not even the roughest cow puncher or mountaineer will allude to it in his presence."[7]

And finally, we have this account from Ellery's friend and co-worker, R.R. Cummings, who was there to help Ellery bury Mattie:

"Mr. Culver brought his wife, then suffering with tuberculosis, and his baby girl, to live in Firehole Basin, hoping the change in climate might benefit her. Her death occurred after a short sojourn there. At that time the snow was on an average of five feet deep and the nearest doctor nineteen miles away, at the Government Post at one of the springs. It was my custom to visit the several hotels under construction at least once in two weeks. Our mode of traveling being on skis. My line man, Joe Folsom, accompanied me. Finding the sick wife dead, we were compelled to remove a partition in order to secure boards with which to make a coffin. The grave was hewn down into the frozen lava formation and after two days hard work, she was consigned to rest, far away from home and friends.

"The wonderful character of this strong brave man, his Christian fortitude and fidelity enabled him to remain and endure uttering no word of complaint, 'She's only gone to sleep and we will soon meet again.' Alone, caring for his little baby girl, (he) remained at Firehole until late in April, when teams were able to reach, and bring them back to friends."[8]

These narratives help us visualize the events surrounding Mattie's death. Sometime after the new year, her respiratory troubles deepened. As February passed, she became more congested. Ellery may have sent for the doctor—who was 19 miles away, at Norris Geyser Basin—to see if he could bring any relief to Mattie. The doctor, knowing Mattie was in the final stages of tuberculosis, might have been able to help relieve her symptoms but not cure her.

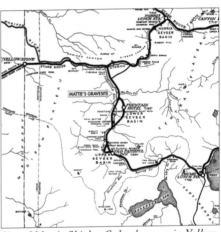

As March began and the snow grew deeper, Ellery certainly could see that Mattie had no chance of recovery. They probably discussed what would be best for Theda's future. Ellery's sister, Laura Culver Bucklin Tyler, and her

Site of Mattie Shipley Culver's grave in Yellowstone National Park.

husband and family had moved to a stock ranch near Lemhi, Idaho in 1882. Maybe they could take Theda.

The Alston family in Spokane was another place Theda would be welcomed. Millie had always been there for Mattie when she was young, and her own children could be companions for Theda. Mattie's mother would help provide grandmotherly love and comfort as well.

Sending Theda to Spokane seemed most logical, and it would allow Ellery to visit without traveling too far. Certainly, it would soothe Mattie to know that her only child would be well cared for and not separated from her family. And Ellery also must have found comfort in a solution that would please Mattie.

When Mattie died, the soldiers at the station across the river tried to help. They took Ellery two empty barrels so that Mattie's body would be safe until it could be buried properly. They placed the barrels end to end and covered them with snow to keep predators from disturbing her body.

Shortly thereafter, Dick (R.R.) Cummings and another employee, Joe Folsom, arrived in the Lower Basin on skis. They

knew Ellery would not be able to rest until Mattie was buried, and so helped for two days, in sub-zero weather, to dig the grave beside the hotel. Then, after making a proper coffin from a partition in the hotel or one of its outbuildings, they performed a brief service to honor Mattie and lowered

R.R. Cummings and Joe Folsom traveled on skis, like the men in the Schwatka expedition of 1887. F.J. Haynes photo at Obsidian Cliff, Montana Historical Society.

her into her resting place, where she will always be remembered by friends and strangers alike.

Completely alone for the next two months, Ellery catered to Theda's every need. Surely this bonding time would help them remain close, no matter how many miles might separate them in the future. For the remainder of the winter, the freshly dug grave would be a daily reminder of the sorrow Ellery must endure. Communication with his family would have helped him through his grieving.

By late April, the Association teams were able to reach Ellery and Theda and get them out of the park. The Culvers then traveled to Spokane, where Theda was welcomed into her new home. Like her own parents, Theda would not be raised by her mother and father. But here she would have companionship, care, plenty of attention and, most important, living memories of her mother.

Through the years, even as the charge of the park has changed, many have cared for and maintained the gravestone with the single rose on it.[9] Ten years before Mattie's death, a friend from Cohoes, Wright W. Skidmore, wrote in her autograph book: "May angels twine bright roses around thy cross." Perhaps roses were Mattie's favorite flower.

Wright W. Skidmore, a friend of Mattie's from Cohoes, New York, penned this wish in her autograph book ten years before Mattie's death.

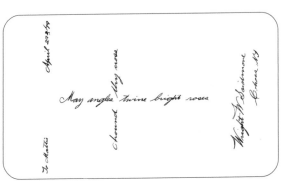

[1] Eruptions of Excelsior Geyser also were reported in 1890 and 1901; Lee Hale Whittlesey, *Wonderland Nomenclature: A History of the Place Names of Yellowstone Park* (Records Management Bureau, Department of Administration; Helena: State of Montana, 1989, text-fiche), pp. 486-492, 8F26-9F6.

[2] "Local News," *The Weekly Gazette*, Billings, Montana; Thursday, 6 September 1888.

[3] "Local News," *The Weekly Gazette*, Billings, Montana; Thursday, 25 October 1888.

[4] "Local News," *The Weekly Gazette*, Billings, Montana; Thursday, 8 November 1888.

[5] *The Livingston Enterprise*, Livingston, Montana; 9 March 1889.

[6] Aubrey L. Haines, *The Yellowstone Story, Volume 2* (Yellowstone National Park, Wyoming: Yellowstone Library and Museum Association, Colorado Associated University Press, 1977), p. 23.

[7] Carl E. Schmidt, *A Western Trip*, (Detroit: Herold Press, 1910), pp. 11-12.

[8] Lee Whittlesey, Yellowstone National Park archivist, believes Joe Folsom may be John Fossum who was the winterkeeper in 1887 at Canyon Hotel.

[9] Information supplied by Aubrey L. Haines.

Epilogue
A Family Remembered

After Mattie died and Theda was safely in Spokane, Ellery went back to work for the Yellowstone Park Association. He never lived in Billings again; instead, he split his time between Yellowstone National Park, Gardiner and Livingston, Montana.

Ellery preserved Mattie's memory well. In 1891, the Fountain Hotel was built a few miles from the obsolete Firehole Hotel. I can imagine Ellery watching as the old hotel and its outbuildings (except for the two cottages he helped build in 1887) were burned. But Ellery saw to it that no harm came to the final resting place of his wife.

On April 12, 1892, Ellery took the oath of office as United States Commissioner of the park, whose charge it was to handle legal wrongdoings within Yellowstone's boundaries. Still, he often found time to visit Theda in Spokane. One of those visits likely occurred after her grandmother, Elizabeth Shipley, died of pneumonia on November 30, 1892.

When the Lacey Act provided for the commissioner's post to become full-time on June 20, 1894, Ellery gave up his position to John W. Meldrum and refocused his efforts with the Yellowstone Park Transportation Company.

On October 14, 1897—perhaps needing a change—Ellery became postmaster of Gardiner, Montana and ran a small grocery called the Postoffice Store. But it was during this time that his health began to fail. At fifty-five, Ellery had frequent bouts of rheumatism: In February, 1904, and again in March, Ellery had severe attacks. The newspaper said he was "almost helpless." As a result of his ill health, Ellery was forced to relinquish his store and his job as postmaster. He spent nearly two months in the house of Millie, Lida, and sixteen-year-old Theda. It was like seeing live reflections of Mattie and hearing echoes of her voice. The care and company of these women helped Ellery regain his strength, and he was back in Gardiner by May 28 to work as runner for the transportation company. He would encourage passengers on the train between Livingston and Cinnabar to use the transportation and accommodations of the Park Association. He was their *color* and undoubtedly good at it.

Theda and the Alstons visited Ellery in Yellowstone too. Lida fell in love with a man from Illinois, where they planned to go to live. On August 11, 1904, Lida wrote to her niece, Grace Alston, about her wedding to Bernie Stamp in Rankin, Illinois and included this about Ellery: "I have sent the news to Ellery. I know he will do something handsome for me: don't you?" In the same letter, she commented about a trip that the family had taken to the park: "Have you heard from Alfred Jr.? You will write him an account of your Wonderland trip, of course." Lida was still making use of underlining for her emphasis like she had in Mattie's autograph book so many years before.

Ellery dabbled in various other enterprises, including traveling to show stereopticon views of the park. He may even have traveled as far as Ohio. There are reminiscences in Lyme township, where Ellery's father moved the family after Ellery's mother's death, that still refer to "seeing slides of the 'Wonders of the Yellowstone.'"[1] In yet another venture, Ellery teamed with A.W. Miles in 1905 to tour the Pacific Coast and exhibit the petrified mummy of a man they claimed was the late territorial governor of Montana, General Thomas Meagher. A cowboy had found the body in the Marias River, near Fort Benton. Meagher had been shot and then thrown into the river years earlier.

Throughout this rambling time, Ellery retained his position with the Park Association, keeping a close watch on Theda and the Alston family. On February 23, 1905, while Ellery was tour-ing, David Alston died, leaving Millie to care for their children and niece. Theda finished high school and was going on to col-lege. It seemed that perhaps she would follow in the footsteps of her Aunt Lida—who began teaching in 1882—and her cousin Grace and become a teacher.

But it was not to be. In the summer of 1906, Theda became ill. Ellery was there for her but she died on July 20, just nineteen years old. From a taped interview with Lena Potter of Gardiner on April 20, 1962, historian Aubrey Haines records her recollec-tion of Ellery's response to Theda's death: ". . . .She was in her teens when she died. That fixed Mr. Culver; he just couldn't gather himself up. . . ."

Theda was buried in the Alston family plot in Fairmount Cemetery in Spokane, beside her grandmother, Elizabeth Shipley.

For the next three years, Ellery lived and worked in Gar-diner. But in 1909, he moved to the Sawtelle National Home for Disabled Volunteer Soldiers in California because he no longer could care for himself. His sister, Laura Culver Bucklin Tyler, had moved from Idaho to Los Angeles, so he had family nearby.

Ellery spent the rest of his life at the veterans facility and, when he was near death, got help from other residents. Sanford Harner stated that he had, "done work for Ellery C. Culver for more than eight months . . . by taking care of his bed and the other work that was needed . . . as he is so crippled up in his hands and feet that he is unable to attend to the things that are necessary to his welfare and comfort. . . ."[2] By November of 1921, Ellery's eyesight was so poor that he discontinued newspaper subscriptions because he no longer could read.

Ellery Channing Culver died April 17, 1922. R.R. Cummings was with him at the time of his death and wrote this:

> "The day before he died, I sat by his bedside. What a change, I said to him. The sun will soon be shining, so we can go out and talk over old times. Tears came into his eyes, and in a feeble and quavering voice he replied: 'Oh, no Dick, I am going to a better home. God has pointed the way, and I am ready to go and meet my maker and

my beloved in heaven.' A true friend and comrade has gone to rest, and I shall miss him, but what an example for us to follow."

Ellery was buried in the National Soldier's Home Cemetery; his grave is among the thousands that stand, row upon row, in what now is downtown Los Angeles. The crowded starkness of the city is such a contrast to the single beauty of Mattie's grave on Nez Perce Creek in Yellowstone National Park. Two lovers buried worlds apart, yet so close together.

Millie no doubt was heartbroken when Theda died, but she continued to be the rock in the family. Her daughter, Grace, remembers Millie years later, when a close friend died and wrote in her diary: "Dr. Harper was lovely. He said the right things. I like the way he distinguishes between a mother and a 'motherly mother,' the kind Mrs. Hansen was and the kind I had." Millie had yet another death to cope with when her daughter, Mildred, died from pneumonia on April 28, 1916.

Ellery Culver in California shortly before his death.

Certainly, Millie looked after her two remaining children carefully after so much tragedy. She must have been proud of them. Grace had become a teacher, and her only son, Edward, was a clerk. Grace married Ernest Hedrick, a railroad man, on November 24, 1917. The small ceremony was in front of the window at the Alston home. Millie lived with the Hedricks until she died of tuberculous peritonitis on June 18, 1923. She is buried next to David on the family plot in Fairmount Cemetery.

When jobs became difficult to find, Edward Alston moved to California to work in one of the government programs. Correspondence between him and Grace documents troublesome times. He worked for a sugar company near Sacramento for a while, then stayed in the Sacramento area for many years. In 1938, his letters took on an air of despair:

"Dear Grace:
    I just received your last letter and thanks for the $5.00. I'm keeping acc't of everything and hope to be able to soon start repaying. . . . We are having showers, but no floods at present, but will have one later on, as there is plenty of snow in the mountains. I look for an early spring and will get into the country as soon as any work starts.
    "I received a letter a few days ago from the S.R.A. saying there would be no W.P.A. work or dole, but to appear and sign up to go to a transient camp. There is no pay and I'd have to associate with the scum of the world and come out as poor as I went in, so I'll stick in the old shack another 3 or 4 weeks and then see what I can do. We get beans from a cleaning mill and rice from another place, so with the cash you send, I'm getting along all right. . . .
                                        Your loving brother Ed."

In another letter on March 25, 1938, he wrote:

"Dear Grace:
    . . . We have had steady rains and high water all month. The whole country around here is mud and water, with the rivers all at flood stage. . . . I'm staying healthy, but have had a lot of blues. A little sunshine will cure that. Tell Ernest hello.
                                        Your loving brother Ed."

Grace followed that letter with one of her own, but it was returned, "unclaimed." She tried to locate Edward through Sacramento County, unsuccessfully, then took a trip to California. This letter was sent to her from the coroner of Sacramento County on May 23, 1938:

"Dear Madam:
    Your letter of May 21st, 1938 from Yuba City informing me of your belief that the body of an unknown white

man found in the Sacramento River on May 14th, 1938 is that of your brother Edward Shipley Alston, received.

"I am enclosing herewith Authority to Cremate blanks in duplicate and if you feel sure enough from your investigation that the deceased is your brother, please sign these and return to me. . . .

"I am also enclosing herewith a letter of authorization to exhume the body and have same cremated which I request you to sign and return to me along with the other papers.

"Upon receipt of these documents properly executed, I will instruct Miller & Skelton to proceed and have your wishes carried out. . . ."

The spring of 1938 brought much sorrow to the Hedrick household. Grace and Ernest had no children, and now the brother they tried to help was dead.

They lived at the house on Chelan Street until Grace died in 1955. Ernest sold the house shortly thereafter to pay hospital bills. He died in 1958.

Mattie's brother, William, and his wife, Electa, had two children, both of whom died in infancy. Electa died in 1917, and William then lived alone but remained active, mostly in church affairs. Even as the mills of Cohoes began to fail, William stayed in the Cohoes area and become a baker. He had been sick for some time before his death in Cohoes on July 4, 1922. Lida was with him when he died and was the informant on the death certificate. William and Electa lie side by side and next to their children in Albany Rural Cemetery.

Lida Shipley Stamp was widowed in 1909, after just five years of marriage. She returned to Spokane to live with Millie for a short time. But she married again in 1911 to John Hurley, also from Rankin, Illinois, and moved to Peoria, Illinois. John was an engineer for the Nickel Plate Railroad. Although Lida and John had no children of their own, Lida treated John's children from his first marriage, Jesse and Hazel, as her own. She was older than both her husbands, which apparently made her a bit uncomfortable; when she married John Hurley, she claimed her birth date was 1868 rather than 1858.

Lida lived the rest of her life in Peoria. She fit into the society there well, becoming a member of the Order of Eastern Star and of Hope Division, No. 10 Auxiliary of the Brotherhood of Locomotive Engineers. Lida outlived all her siblings and most of her nieces and nephews. She died January 16, 1932 and is buried in Parkview Memorial Cemetery in Peoria. Her husband, John, died in 1939, and is buried beside her.

Mattie's aunt, Martha Platt, died in Lowell, Massachusetts in 1894, just two years after her sister died in Spokane. There now remain no living descendants of George and Elizabeth Shipley, who came to America to begin a new life in 1849.

---

[1] Adeline Wright, *Life in Lyme* (Historic Lyme Village Association, 1976), p. 28.

[2] Military pension papers of Ellery C. Culver.

---— *Afterword* ---—

People often ask why I put so much time into something that doesn't have any connection to me. But I actually have many connections to Mattie, however subtle they may seem. I also found that many other people feel the need to know the story of Mattie's life.

Mattie may have lived only a short time, but her spirit lives on in Yellowstone today. And while her life may appear tragic to some, it also was full of happiness, friendship, bravery and beauty.

The parallels between Mattie's early life and my own helped me identify with her. I also lost my parents at a young age and lived with siblings as I grew up. And I moved often when I was a child, learning that change could be stimulating.

Like Mattie, I later chose to move away from the area where I grew up. There always seemed to be more out there, and I enjoyed searching for it. Yellowstone National Park became a focal point in my life as well. Mattie's time in the park sparked my interest in the history of the area and its people; they continue to teach us today.

My love for the forest and the life within it grew as I hiked the oldest trails I could find surrounding Mattie's gravesite. As soon as you get away from the crowded road system in Yellowstone, it's easy to understand why Mattie chose to share the time with Ellery in the park rather than wait in Billings. Besides, she was not a "waiter."

So, when people ask why I've spent so much time and effort on this endeavor, I remind them how much we can learn from the past and its people: Daily behavior matters; I care about the consequences of actions, of choices; each of us is responsible for our actions, and people and nature are not separate from each other; life can be good even after major disruptions; looking for happiness is part of life, and even after death, a life can hold meaning for those who follow.

Mattie's gravestone has led me to important friendships I might otherwise never have found. For those people I have met in the course of this research and for others who I now appreciate more than ever before, I thank you, Mattie.

The next time it seems as if someone is speaking to you from the grave, pay attention to the voice. Maybe someone wants to share a lifetime of experience with you.

12TH CENSUS OF THE UNITED STATES NO. 1 - POPULATION State of Washington, Spokane Co. Spokane City Ward 4

Enumerated by me on the Fifth day of June, 1900, George Watkins, Enumerator   903 Chelan Street

Group	#	Description	Alston, David	Alston, Millie	Alston, Grace E.	Alston, Edward S.	Alston, Mildred	Culver, Theda	Shipley, Lida
Locations	1	Number of dwelling-house in the order of visitation	111						
Locations	2	Number of family in the order of visitation	117						
Name	3	Name of each person whose place of abode on June 1, 1900 was in this family. Enter surname first, then the given name and middle initial, if any. Include every person living on June 1, 1900. Omit children born since June 1, 1900	Alston, David	Alston, Millie	Alston, Grace E.	Alston, Edward S.	Alston, Mildred	Culver, Theda	Shipley, Lida
Relation	4	Relationship of each person to the head of the family	Head	Wife	Daughter	Son	Daughter	Niece	Sister
Personal Description	5	Color or race	W	W	W	W	W	W	W
Personal Description	6	Sex	M	F	F	M	F	F	F
Personal Description	7	Date of Birth Month/Year	Jan 1844	Sep 1847	May 1882	Apr 1884	Nov 1886	June 1887	Oct 1858
Personal Description	8	Age at last birthday	56	52	18	16	13	12	41
Personal Description	9	Whether single, married, widowed, or divorced	M	M	S	S	S	S	S
Personal Description	10	Number of years married	19	19					
Personal Description	11	Mother of how many children		4					
Personal Description	12	Number of these children living		3					
Nativity (Place of birth of each person and parents of each person enumerated. If born in the United States, give the State or Territory; if of foreign birth, give the Country only.)	13	Place of birth of this PERSON	New York	England	Montana	Montana	Wash	Montana	Mass
Nativity	14	Place of birth of FATHER of this person	New York	England	New York	New York	New York	New York	England
Nativity	15	Place of birth of MOTHER of this person	Ireland	England	England	England	England	England	England
Citizenship	16	Year of migration to the United States		1848					
Citizenship	17	Number of years in the United States		51					
Citizenship	18	Naturalization							
Occupation, trade or profession (of each person ten years of age and over)	19	Occupation	Mining		At school	At school	At school	At school	Teacher
Occupation, trade or profession	20	Months not employed	5						0
Education	21	Attended school (in months)			9	9	9	9	
Education	22	Can read	Yes	Yes	Yes	Yes	Yes	Yes	Yes
Education	23	Can write	Yes	Yes	Yes	Yes	Yes	Yes	Yes
Education	24	Can speak English	Yes	Yes	Yes	Yes	Yes	Yes	Yes